FISCAL POLICY AND SUSTAINABLE FINANCE

ENHANCING THE ROLE OF THE FINANCIAL SECTOR IN
ACHIEVING THE SUSTAINABLE DEVELOPMENT GOALS

JUNE 2024

ASIAN DEVELOPMENT BANK

ADB

© 2024 Asian Development Bank
6 ADB Avenue, Mandaluyong City, 1550 Metro Manila, Philippines
Tel +63 2 8632 4444; Fax +63 2 8636 2444
www.adb.org

Some rights reserved. Published in 2024.

ISBN 978-92-9270-715-6 (print); 978-92-9270-716-3 (PDF); 978-92-9270-717-0 (e-book)
Publication Stock No. TCS240284-2
DOI: http://dx.doi.org/10.22617/TCS240284-2

Notes:
In this publication, "$" refers to United States dollars, "€" refers to euros, "HK$" refers to Hong Kong dollars, "RM" refers to Malaysian ringgit, and "SKr" refers to Swedish kronor.
ADB recognizes "China" as the People's Republic of China; "Hong Kong" as Hong Kong, China; and "Korea" as the Republic of Korea.

Cover design by Claudette Rodrigo.

Printed on recycled paper

Contents

Tables and Figures

Acknowledgments

Fiscal Policy and Sustainable Finance: Enhancing the Role of the Financial Sector in Achieving Sustainable Development Goals is a product of the Sectors Group of the Asian Development Bank (ADB).

We thank Christine Engstrom, senior director of the Finance Sector under Sectors Group (SG-FIN), for the support and guidance in crafting this report. The report was authored by Zalina Shamsudin of Climate Bonds Initiative, who provided the expertise and knowledge needed to develop this report. Dudi Rulliadi and Haryadi from the Fiscal Policy Office of the Ministry of Finance Indonesia led the refining work of the report with comments and inputs from the financial authorities of the Association of Southeast Asian Nations plus the People's Republic of China, Japan, and the Republic of Korea. Raquel Borres, senior economics officer, SG-FIN, led the effort to coordinate and contribute to the development and production of the report. Junkyu Lee, director, SG-FIN, provided overall directions, valuable feedback, and inputs and supervised its production. Special thanks go to Xiaoqin Fan, director, SG-FIN, who reviewed the report without sparing hard effort to enhance the report's quality and proper structure. We are also very grateful for the input of selected individuals from finance ministries, investment companies, and issuers in the Association of Southeast Asian Nations region to the interview and survey. The report was produced with the support of a team of ADB consultants comprising Eric Van Zant as editor, Levi Rodolfo Lusterio as proofreader, Alfred De Jesus for typeset and layout, and Claudette Rodrigo for the graphics design of the cover. Katherine Mitzi Co, associate operations analyst, SG-FIN, and Matilde Mila Cauinian, operations assistant, SG-FIN, provided valuable administrative support. ADB greatly acknowledges all these contributions.

Abbreviations

ADB	Asian Development Bank
ASEAN	Association of Southeast Asian Nations
ASEAN+3	Association of Southeast Asian Nations Plus Three
ESG	environmental, social, and governance
EU	European Union
GSS+	green, social, sustainability, sustainability-linked, and other thematic
MSME	micro, small and medium-sized enterprise
SRI	sustainable and responsible investment
UK	United Kingdom

I.   The Need for Sustainable Finance

Without rapid climate action, countries face severe climate impacts, rising capital costs, and stunted growth. Indeed, the Intergovernmental Panel on Climate Change makes it clear that anthropogenic climate change is already generating severe physical impacts.

Limiting average global warming to above preindustrial levels of 1.5°C is crucial to prevent catastrophic human, ecological, and financial impacts (Figure 1). While this remains in reach, the window for action is rapidly closing.[1]

The cost of capital is already being impacted by physical climate risks, costing the so-called Vulnerable 20 nations $62 billion in higher interest payments from 2008 to 2018.[2] Transition risks are materializing for countries most reliant on fossil fuel exports. From 2015 to 2020, two of the 20 most-exposed sovereigns defaulted, while they experienced an average credit rating downgrade of 1.6 notches.[3]

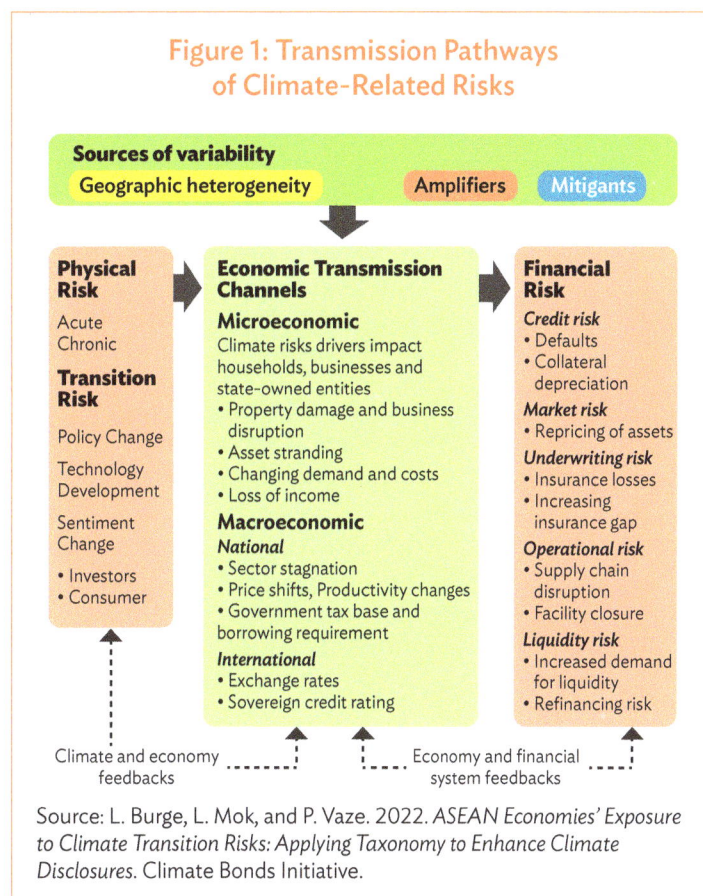

Figure 1: Transmission Pathways of Climate-Related Risks

Sources of variability
Geographic heterogeneity   Amplifiers   Mitigants

Physical Risk
Acute
Chronic

Transition Risk
Policy Change
Technology Development
Sentiment Change
• Investors
• Consumer

Economic Transmission Channels
Microeconomic
Climate risks drivers impact households, businesses and state-owned entities
• Property damage and business disruption
• Asset stranding
• Changing demand and costs
• Loss of income
Macroeconomic
National
• Sector stagnation
• Price shifts, Productivity changes
• Government tax base and borrowing requirement
International
• Exchange rates
• Sovereign credit rating

Financial Risk
Credit risk
• Defaults
• Collateral depreciation
Market risk
• Repricing of assets
Underwriting risk
• Insurance losses
• Increasing insurance gap
Operational risk
• Supply chain disruption
• Facility closure
Liquidity risk
• Increased demand for liquidity
• Refinancing risk

Climate and economy feedbacks   Economy and financial system feedbacks

Source: L. Burge, L. Mok, and P. Vaze. 2022. *ASEAN Economies' Exposure to Climate Transition Risks: Applying Taxonomy to Enhance Climate Disclosures*. Climate Bonds Initiative.

Delayed emissions reductions, i.e., after 2030, would demand far stronger policies and sudden changes in technology and likely breach several climate tipping points. This so-called disorderly transition would, therefore, increase physical and transition risk exposure (Figure 2).[4]

---

[1]   Intergovernmental Panel on Climate Change. 2021. *Climate Change 2021: The Physical Science Basis*. Contribution of Working Group I to the Sixth Assessment Report of the Intergovernmental Panel on Climate Change. https://www.ipcc.ch/report/ar6/wg1/.

[2]   B. Buhr, U. Volz, C. Donovan, G. Kling, Y.C. Lo, V. Murinde, and N. Pullin. 2018. *Climate Change and the Cost of Capital in Developing Countries*. UN Environment. https://eprints.soas.ac.uk/26038.

[3]   Fitch Ratings. 2021. *Special Report: Climate Change "Stranded Assets" Area Long-Term Risk for Some Sovereigns*. https://www.fitchratings.com/research/sovereigns/climate-change-stranded-assets-are-long-term-risk-for-some-sovereigns-15-02-2021. A rating notch is the difference between a rating and the next rating down, for example, BB+ and BB.

[4]   NGFS Climate Scenarios for Central Banks and Supervisors. https://www.ngfs.net/en/ngfs-climate-scenarios-central-banks-and-supervisors-september-2022.

Figure 2: Annual Carbon Dioxide Emissions and Global Temperature Change under the Network for Greening the Financial System's Orderly and Disorderly Transition Scenarios

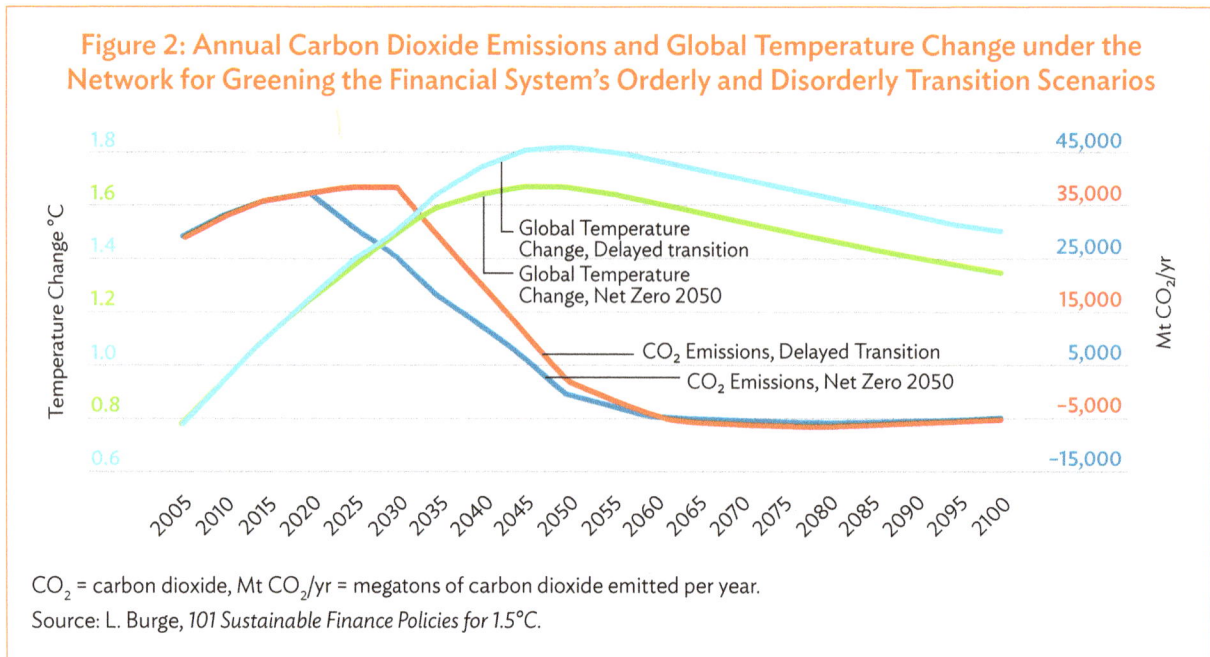

CO$_2$ = carbon dioxide, Mt CO$_2$/yr = megatons of carbon dioxide emitted per year.
Source: L. Burge, *101 Sustainable Finance Policies for 1.5°C.*

In addition, slow transition will be more expensive than rapid transition. Immediate action will result in significant savings because renewables are already less expensive than fossil fuels. This is without including avoided climate damage expenses or any other economic co-benefits from climate action.[5]

A slow transition will limit development opportunities and reduce countries' prosperity, particularly for those lagging. This is because countries taking rapid action will likely attract more investment, disrupt trade and supply chains in their favor, and decrease demand for fossil fuels.

Meeting 1.5°C Requires Major Reallocation to Green Private Investment

Globally, by 2030, climate finance will need to have increased six times to more than $4 trillion by 2030 (Figure 3). Closing this net-zero investment gap will require enormous crowding in private investment.[6]

Enough capital is available to close the investment gap; bond markets alone have around $130 trillion outstanding.[7] However, investment models and decision-making processes do not fully incorporate climate risks and opportunities. Historical and/or short-term analysis tends to underestimate climate opportunities and overvalue fossil fuel investments, due to lack of precedent for the former and strong historical performance by the latter.

[5]   R. Way, M.C. Ives, P. Mealy, and J. Doyne Farmer. 2022. Empirically Grounded Technology Forecasts and the Energy Transition. *Joule.* 6 (9). pp. 2057–2082. https://doi.org/10.1016/j.joule.2022.08.009.

[6]   Climate Policy Initiative. 2021. *Global Landscape of Climate Finance 2021.* https://www.climatepolicyinitiative.org/publication/global-landscape-of-climate-finance-2021/.

[7]   ICMA. n.d. *Bond Market Size.* https://www.icmagroup.org/market-practice-and-regulatory-policy/secondary-markets/bond-market-size/.

Figure 3: Net-Zero Investment Gap

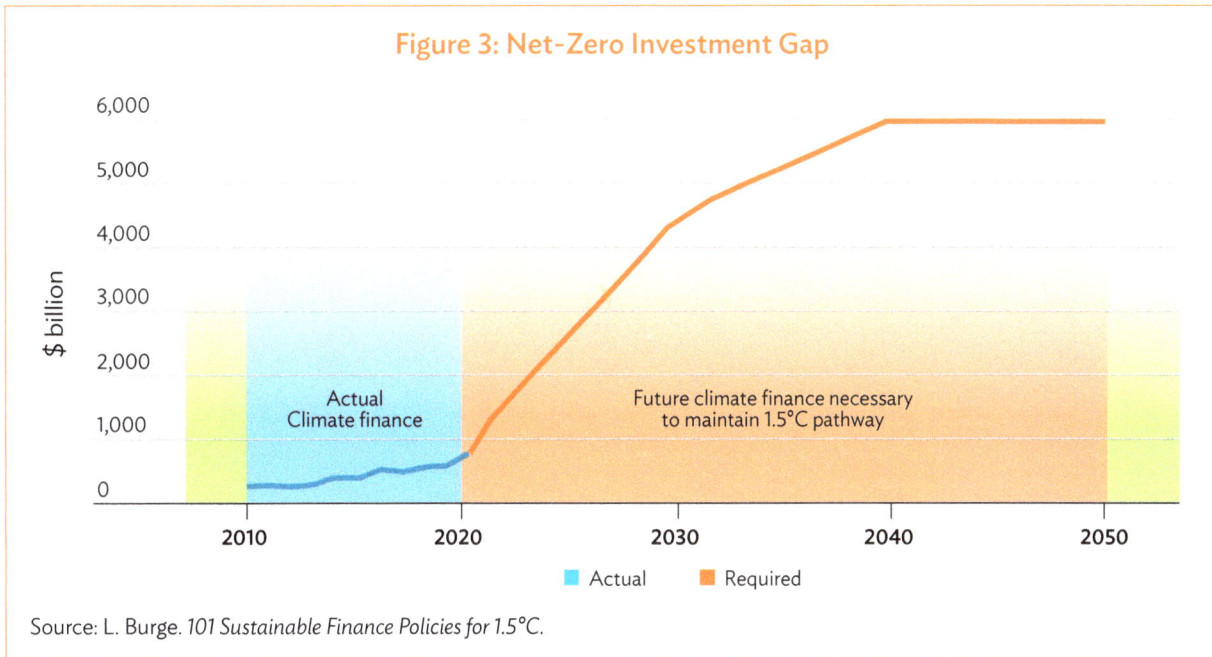

Source: L. Burge. *101 Sustainable Finance Policies for 1.5°C.*

Demand for green investments is very high. However, investors' risk appetites do not match many of the key sustainable investments needed to meet 1.5°C, such as in new technologies or developing economies. If this risk is not addressed, financial markets cannot deliver deep decarbonization, which may exacerbate existing inequalities. Policies are required to reduce both real and perceived risks of climate investments.

Overly Complex Sustainable Investment Procedures Could Slow Transition

Lack of transparency or clarity over what makes a credible climate investment can disincentivize such investment due to greenwashing concerns or insufficient knowledge and capacity among investors for green credibility assessment. Policymakers and regulators are, therefore, crucial to enabling investment and providing guidance and financial structures such as green taxonomies.

Sustainable investments can be substantially more complicated than other investments, owing to additional due diligence and regulation. This would discourage investors without specific green investment mandates, meaning capital will not move at scale. Simplicity must be prioritized in all policies.

Coordinated Fiscal Policies Are Vital to Sustainable Finance Policies to Help Meet 1.5°C

Fiscal policies are central to driving sustainable development, as they influence all of the real and financial economic sectors and generally can directly address the barriers to the flow of sustainable finance. Taxation, expenditure allocation, and government borrowing structures can tilt economies toward green opportunities and sustainability.

Climate action and the development of sustainable finance can also enable finance ministries to achieve their core responsibilities: macroeconomic stability, growth, and responsible public finance management.[8] A wide variety of policies is available to these ministries, which will overcome the barriers preventing private and public capital from flowing toward sustainable projects and investments. They can be categorized into three broad purposes: ensuring speed of action, steering toward a green economy, and simplifying investment decisions (Table 1).

Table 1: Sustainable Finance Policy Options Available to Ministries of Finance

Type	Speed: Ensure Rapid Action	Steer: Tilt Economy to Deliver Transition		Simplify: Streamline Sustainable Investment
		Incorporate transition risk and opportunity	De-risk green opportunities	
Direct impact on financial sector	• Sustainable finance roadmap • Sustainable central bank mandate/remit	• Green sovereign wealth fund	• Tax incentives • Green guarantees • Green finance subsidies • Sovereign-to-sovereign guarantees	• GSS+ sovereign issuance
Indirect impact on financial sector, transmitted through real economy		• Carbon pricing • Green public investment management • Environmental tax reform • Fossil fuel subsidy phaseout		

GSS = green, social, sustainable, and sustainability linked.
Source: Adapted from L. Burge. 2023. *101 Sustainable Finance Policies for 1.5°C*. Climate Bonds Initiative. https://www.climatebonds.net/resources/reports/101-sustainable-finance-policies-15%C2%B0c-0.

This paper delves into the design, development, and implementation of fiscal policies that directly impact the financial sector. It highlights the experiences of successful policies in recent years in the Association of Southeast Asian Nations plus three (ASEAN+3) countries and implementation challenges, to provide a wide range of recommendations for policymaking.[9]

A.   Research Methodology

Rather than an exhaustive analysis of all relevant sustainability policies, the report chose a research methodology that prioritizes a focus on financial policies identified as effective. It highlights case studies of specific successful policies. Focusing on these policies rather than on markets deemed successful and reviewing their policies avoids bias and recognizes that other external factors might drive a country's success. As part of the research methodology, the report provides evidence of success in reinforcing the choice of policies.

Table 1 highlights policy interventions for closer scrutiny. These interventions have been extracted from the Climate Bonds Initiative's paper *101 Sustainable Finance Policies for 1.5°C*.[10]

---

[8]   Finance Ministers for Climate. 2023. *Strengthening the Role of Ministries of Finance in Driving Climate Action*. https://www.financeministersforclimate.org/sites/cape/files/inline-files/Summary%20Strengthening%20the%20Role%20of%20Finance%20Ministries.pdf.
[9]   The 10 members of the Association of Southeast Asian Nations plus the People's Republic of China, Japan, and the Republic of Korea.
[10]   Climate Bonds Initiative. *101 Sustainable Finance Policies for 1.5°C*. https://www.climatebonds.net/policy/101-policymakers.

This report identifies policies that directly affect financial sector development, as this would more immediately widen sustainable finance availability and disbursements. However, the full success of such policies does depend on the implementation of supportive real economy policies.

B.   Assessment Methodology

Given the approach used to research and analyze the implementation effectiveness of pre-identified and proven policies on sustainable finance growth, the paper uses the following assessment methodology:

Stage 1: Identify policies considered more impactful than others.

Stage 2: Map the existence of these policies in ASEAN+3 countries.

Stage 3: Confirm the presence of the policies using the following assessment metrics:

- **Status of policy:** In force, proposed, development.
- **Comprehensiveness:** National or regional impact, economy-wide or sectoral coverage.

Stage 4: Determine if there were common gaps or barriers in the effectiveness of policy implementation/uptake:

- **Structural issues**, for example:
    - micro, small, and medium-sized enterprise (MSME) predominance,
    - different regulations and definitions in different regions,
    - risk aversion, and
    - fossil fuel incumbents.
- **Political:** Lack of government support or lack of integration between ministries—contradictory policies.
- **Policy design:** Flaws in the design of policies such as:
    - a mismatch between financial structures used and policy supports (i.e., if a loan-reliant economy and subsidies focus on bonds),
    - weakness in green definitions,
    - administrative complexity of applying for subsidy schemes and confusion over eligibility for different schemes, and
    - long permitting time for renewable energy installations (for example, land use conversion and connection to the main electricity grid).
- **Knowledge:**
    - lack of capacity and technical expertise in government, the real economy, and the financial sector; and
    - underestimation of climate-related financial risks.
- **Pipeline:** Lack of project pipeline or mismatch between projects and investor demand.

Stage 4 analysis will be based on interview feedback and responses to survey questions. Appendix 2 reflects the proposed stakeholders identified for interviews and proposed questions.

II. Fiscal Policies to Mobilize Sustainable Finance

Finance ministries are increasingly recognizing the crucial role of the financial system in delivering climate mitigation and adaptation, as well as sustainable development. By adjusting government expenditure and revenue collection, fiscal policymakers can encourage investment in climate-aligned sectors and technologies and support sustainable low-carbon growth.

Certain policies have been identified as a priority for ASEAN+3, which will enable the rapid development of the sustainable finance market. These policies have been selected based on the analysis of the long-term impact each policy has had on domestic financial sector growth in sustainability, as seen in developed markets (Table 2). This is not necessarily the optimal combination of policies to be implemented, but rather a list of policy options.

Table 2: Definitions of Policies Recommended

Sustainable finance policy roadmap	Such roadmaps set out the government's approach and definition of sustainable finance and outline policy intentions. They can help prioritize actions, coordinate stakeholders, and secure buy-in from market participants. Detailed roadmaps can set out specific timelines for policy implementation, providing future guidance for investors and project developers.
Green/sustainable tax incentives	Such incentives are financial benefits, including tax exemptions and accelerated depreciation that reduce the tax burden to encourage climate investments.
Green sovereign guarantees	Assurances against country-level risks are essential in developing and emerging markets to enable investments bankable by foreign investors. Sovereign guarantees de-risk investments, increasing confidence in repayment.
Green finance subsidies	Green finance subsidies steer investments towards new market sectors. They can be designed to come in many forms, for example direct payments such as a cash reimbursement of costs of issuances.
Sovereign green, social, sustainability, and sustainability-linked bond issuance	Bonds issued by any sovereign entity. Either use-of-proceeds instruments whereby the proceeds of these bonds are used only for specific green, social, and/or sustainable projects or sustainability-linked bonds; general purpose bonds with sustainability performance targets linked to coupon step up/down or early repayment obligations.

Source: Author.

A.   Sustainable Finance Policy Roadmap

Coordination required: Participation in development and implementation—central bank, regulators, other ministries, and stock exchange. Consultation during development: private sector players, including verifiers, rating agencies, investment banks, and investors

An environment of policy uncertainty can hinder investment flow, with investors unsure of whether policies will be introduced or how long support schemes will last. In addition, policy misalignment between departments, such as on what qualifies as a sustainable investment, can create confusion and inefficiencies.

A roadmap provides certainty on policy introduction, directly encouraging the financial sector to increase sustainable investments. A sustainable finance policy roadmap was seen as the most important policy to unlock sustainable investment by respondents. Roadmap development is one of the strongest signals a ministry of finance can send of its commitment to develop sustainable finance markets.

The roadmap sets out the government's approach and definition of sustainable finance and outlines policy intentions (e.g., disclosure requirements, taxonomy, regulatory requirements). Depending on the granularity, the roadmap can also set out timelines for the implementation of policies. The United Kingdom's (UK) roadmap, for example, clearly sets out the reasoning behind policies and provides a clear timetable for implementation. Its asset manager disclosure requirements will be made mandatory following corporate requirements to ensure data availability.[11]

The combination of policies set out in the roadmap will depend on the local economic and political context, market participant requirements, and existing policies.[12]

A policy roadmap enables coordination between government departments, the central bank, and financial regulators. Cross-government alignment stems from government leadership, but the ministry of finance can ensure day-to-day coordination, such as in the supervision of ministerial and sub-national government budgets. For example, the European Union (EU) Action Plan on Financing Sustainable Growth (or Renewed Sustainable Finance Strategy) was introduced to coordinate the development of the Green Taxonomy and various climate disclosure regulations.[13]

Roadmap development requires strong coordination and commitment among a range of players, including policymakers, industry regulators, and related players in the landscape. For example, Thailand's roadmap was developed by a sustainable finance working group that included the Ministry of Finance, the Securities and Exchange Commission, the Bank of Thailand, the Stock Exchange, and the Office of Insurance Commission.[14] If internal capacity or expertise to develop the roadmap is lacking, the central bank can be enlisted to lead development—as Morocco's central bank did. A multilateral development bank, foreign government, or nongovernment organization can also provide support, as in the Philippines Roadmap.[15]

---

[11]   Government of the UK. 2021. *Greening Finance: A Roadmap to Sustainable Investing.* https://www.gov.uk/government/publications/greening-finance-a-roadmap-to-sustainable-investing.

[12]   Coalition of Finance Ministers for Climate Action and UNDP Financial Centers for Sustainability. 2021. *An Analysis of Sustainable Finance Roadmaps.* https://www.financeministersforclimate.org/news/hp5-publishes-sustainable-finance-roadmaps-report.

[13]   European Commission. 2018. *Renewed Sustainable Finance Strategy and Implementation of the Action Plan on Financing Sustainable Growth.* https://ec.europa.eu/info/publications/sustainable-finance-renewed-strategy_en.

[14]   Bank of Thailand. *Sustainable Finance Initiatives for Thailand.* https://www.bot.or.th/content/dam/bot/financial-innovation/sustainable-finance/green/Sustainable_Finance_Initiatives_for_Thailand.pdf.

[15]   The Philippine Sustainable Finance Roadmap. https://www.dof.gov.ph/wp-content/uploads/2021/10/ALCEP-Roadmap.pdf.

Effective roadmap design will successfully address country-specific market failures that are limiting sustainable investments. This requires the inclusion of key stakeholders, including the ministry of finance, central bank, regulators, technical experts, and other financial actors. This will help ensure realistic goals and buy-in from affected stakeholders. In addition, this early-stage policy dialogue can help develop a pipeline of suitable investments, accelerating action.

When implementing a strategy, it can be challenging if all the stakeholders are not committed to the plan or to implementing the necessary changes. Therefore, in most cases, the ministries of finance are responsible for ensuring that relevant players are on board. To include wider policies, such as green quantitative easing and blended finance, buy-in from other key actors, such as the central bank and development finance institutions, is necessary. It is also crucial to engage continuously with stakeholders and gather feedback during policy implementation to ensure that it remains relevant and effective. Additionally, implementing a governance infrastructure to coordinate various stakeholders can be helpful. This could be in the form of a committee, task force, or working group comprising relevant parties, supported by a strong secretariat. For example, a committee was formed to develop a strong and sustainable finance roadmap, consisting of relevant stakeholders. Unfortunately, the committee fell short in impact as it lacked infrastructure to monitor implementation or provide necessary capacity building for the industry.

Engaging with other countries at the design stage enables roadmap developers to learn from their experience and to align and standardize approaches that can stimulate cross-border finance flows.

Roadmap policies should be achievable and actionable. Inclusive design can contribute to this. In addition, policies should be specific and clear, with specified accountability and responsibility for implementation. Accountability mechanisms, including monitoring, performance indicators, and reporting, ensure momentum and demonstrate commitment that gives investors confidence in policy introduction.

Including capacity building in roadmaps is also crucial to enable financial actors to transform their activities, enabling them to carry out climate risk and opportunity assessments, issue green finance instruments, etc. Capacity building should be available to a wide range of actors to enable the mainstreaming of sustainable finance across the financial system.

Data quality and availability, likewise, are highly important to increasing sustainable investments, as are roadmaps. Roadmaps provide a reliable timeline for introducing disclosure requirements, giving financial actors time to meet them. They can stagger requirements and align with capacity-building programs to account for different actors' disclosure capabilities. Roadmaps will set out the sequencing of policy introductions. Policies can be prioritized by urgency, feasibility, and dependency on other policies.

B.   Tax Incentives

Coordination required: Capital market regulator, ministry of finance, and inland revenue authorities

Investors without a green investment focus will have no particular motivation to invest in green issuance, as market assessments do not fully incorporate climate risks and opportunities. Tax incentives, such as tax exemptions on green bond holdings, can also be used to encourage these investors to increase green investment.

Tax incentives can encourage green, social, sustainability, sustainability-linked, and other thematic (GSS+) issuance, for example, through tax credit bonds, in which the investor receives a tax credit instead of the issuer paying interest. This structure is used for United States municipal bonds. Other examples include stamp duty exemptions for investors and accelerated depreciation for net zero projects.

By setting a limit for issuer and/or investor size eligibility for the incentive, the government can ensure it does not significantly impact the tax base and, hence, may also be phased out once the market reaches maturity or a certain size.

In Malaysia, tax exemption is available for the issuance of GSS+ bonds and *sukuk* issuance. Expanded following the popularity of sustainability-linked instruments, the sustainable and responsible investment (SRI) *Sukuk* and Bond Grant Scheme is also applicable to *sukuk* issuance following the Securities Commission's SRI-linked *Sukuk* Framework and bonds issued under the ASEAN Sustainability-linked Bond Standards, which aims to facilitate companies raising funds to transition to low-carbon activities.[16]

The financial sector can also be impacted by indirect tax incentives which target the real economy. Green investments, such as renewables development, often have very high upfront costs. Tax benefits can address these costs with accelerated depreciation schemes, which allow increased tax deductions during the first years of a project. Financial instrument incentives should be aligned with real economy tax incentives to ensure they are coherent and do not send mixed signals. Existing real economy incentives should also be considered when analyzing the additionality of financial instrument incentives.

Incentives may only be put in place to build the market when it is very underdeveloped. Once the market begins to mature, issuance and/or investment will become appealing in its own right, and the incentive can be phased out. This can also limit the cost of such measures. Clearly communicating phaseout dates and/or conditions will provide the market with confidence.

Tax incentives in the financial sector are considered relatively easy to structure and mobilize. Still, challenges in implementation could arise if tax authorities make paperwork too strenuous to claim the incentive.

C.   Green Sovereign Guarantees

Coordination required: International organizations such as the International Monetary Fund and the World Bank

Green investments can carry higher risks due to the innovative nature of technologies, uncertainty about demand, or concerns around the availability of supporting infrastructure. Investors will, therefore, demand high returns on investment, resulting in a very high cost of capital for project developers.

Government guarantees, including partial risk, first-loss, or liquidity guarantees, provide credit enhancement, de-risking the issuance and increasing investor confidence in repayment. This enables longer-term investor participation and decreases the cost of capital to the project owner as investors will require lower returns investors. Guarantees make more projects viable for private investment, increasing overall green financial flows. Local guarantee provision (by government, national development bank, or green bank) can increase visibility and accessibility to local developers.[17]

---

[16]   Securities Commission Malaysia. 2022. *Expansion of SRI Sukuk and Bond Grant Scheme to Facilitate Sustainable Finance.*
        https://www.sc.com.my/resources/media/media-release/expansion-of-sri-sukuk-and-bond-grant-scheme-to-facilitate-sustainable-finance.
[17]   Climate Policy Initiative. 2019. *Developing a Guarantee Instrument to Catalyze Renewable Energy Investments in Indonesia.* https://www.climatepolicy
        initiative.org/publication/developing-a-guarantee-instrument-to-catalyze-renewable-energy-investments-in-indonesia/.

When creating a green guarantee scheme, it is crucial to have a proper methodology for assessing eligibility. It is recommended to follow international green definitions like the EU's or the Climate Bonds Taxonomy to attract global investors for green-guaranteed investments. For instance, the Green Guarantee Company follows criteria that are in line with the Climate Bonds Standards.[18]

Moreover, the eligibility methodology can also help to drive ambition, such as requiring the entity to have a valid transition plan in place. Other eligibility criteria could be a minimum credit rating to ensure the guarantee can bring the investment to the investment grade. The Green Guarantee Company guarantees investments of B and up.[19] A minimum size could also be applied to ensure that the bond or loan meets investors' demands. For example, the Swedish debt office requires loans to be at least SKr500 million to qualify for a green guarantee.[20]

Guarantee provisions can also be made sector and size-specific to ensure they reach the projects key to transition—general guarantee programs may see renewables outcompeted by other sectors and larger projects. For example, in Indonesia, available guarantee schemes are not sector-specific, and guarantee use has tended to focus on large-scale transactions.[21] In contrast, South Africa's Renewable Energy Independent Power Producer Procurement Program includes sovereign guarantees that backstop government commitments to purchase electricity from independent power producers. This program has been instrumental in attracting private sector investment in renewable energy projects, including wind and solar farms, which has helped diversify South Africa's energy mix and reduce greenhouse gas emissions.

When designing guarantees, the government can coordinate with development banks to ensure complementarity. For example, if a development bank already provides first-loss guarantees for renewable energy investments, the government can prioritize other sectors.

To efficiently use public capital, guarantees should only cover the risks that the market cannot absorb—blanket guarantees covering all investment risks, skewing the market significantly, or "picking winners" should be avoided.[22] The type of guarantee will depend on the risks present in the local economy. Political risk guarantees cover currency risks, conflict, breach of contract, etc.; credit guarantees cover default risks; and public sector performance risk guarantees cover public institution default on financial obligations. In addition, the level of risk coverage will have to be decided (partial/full), as will the fee structure, coverage ratio, and governance structure.[23] These are all explicit guarantees. Implicit guarantee provisions could also raise confidence, but they are not explored here as they do not require specific policymaking.

The InvestEU Fund aims to mobilize over €372 billion in investment with a €26.2 billion EU budget guarantee, 30% of which must support climate investments.[24]

---

[18]   The Green Guarantee Company. *Guarantee Criteria.* https://greenguarantee.co/our-guarantee-process/.

[19]   The Green Guarantee Company. *Problems We Solve.* https://greenguarantee.co/the-problem-we-solve/.

[20]   Swedish National Debt Office. *FAQ - Credit Guarantees for Green Investments.* https://www.riksgalden.se/en/our-operations/guarantee-and-lending/credit-guarantees-for-green-investments/questions-and-answers-about-credit-guarantees-for-green-investments/.

[21]   Climate Policy Initiative. 2019. *Developing a Guarantee Instrument to Catalyze Renewable Energy Investments in Indonesia.* https://www.climatepolicyinitiative.org/publication/developing-a-guarantee-instrument-to-catalyze-renewable-energy-investments-in-indonesia/.

[22]   S. Kidney, P. Oliver, and B. Sonerud. 2014. Greening China's Bond Market. Chapter 10 in *Greening China's Financial System. Winnipeg: International Institute for Sustainable Development.* https://www.iisd.org/system/files/publications/greening-chinas-financial-system-chapter-10.pdf.

[23]   Climate Policy Initiative. 2019. *Developing a Guarantee Instrument to Catalyze Renewable Energy Investments in Indonesia.* 3 June. https://www.climatepolicyinitiative.org/publication/developing-a-guarantee-instrument-to-catalyze-renewable-energy-investments-in-indonesia/.

[24]   European Union. *InvestEU Fund.* https://investeu.europa.eu/what-investeu-programme/investeu-fund_en.

Policy design could include establishing a dedicated green guarantee facility to streamline decision-making, such as the Asian Development Bank's (ADB) Pacific Renewable Energy Programme.[25] A centralized facility can also ensure that guarantees do not exceed balance sheet capacity.[26]

Guarantees come with a liability risk, which is characterized by the uncertainty of the timing and amount of liability. This uncertainty can have an impact on fiscal management. To fulfill their guarantees, the government must have enough liquidity in their balance sheet. Guarantee provision should align with the jurisdiction's prudential risks.

D.   Green Finance Subsidies

Coordination required: Development finance institution, central bank, capital market regulator

Issuance of and investment in green bonds and other sustainable finance instruments can cost more than normal or "plain vanilla" equivalents. This is due to additional due diligence and processes, such as obtaining a second-party opinion and use of proceeds reports. Direct subsidies such as interest rate subsidies or stamp duty exemptions can remove this barrier to issuance and could also cover the cost of external review and verification. These can be targeted to smaller issuers for whom these additional costs are more significant. Depending on the level of subsidy, they could even encourage green over vanilla issuance.

In implementation, stamp duty exemptions and reimbursement of verification costs can be straightforward if the documentation is simple and the approving authority dedicates the right resources to make the process time-efficient. However, interest rate subsidies can be challenging to implement if developers are not creditworthy and thus do not qualify for private sector debt.

Some market participants see the additional costs and effort of GSS+ issuance as a barrier to issuance. Subsidies can directly tackle this by covering the cost of green bond verification and/or external review.

By providing an upper limit to the size of the subsidy provided, policymakers can ensure that use is not dominated by large issuers for whom the cost of verification is proportionally much lower. For example, Malaysia's SRI *Sukuk* and Bond Grant Scheme covers 90% of external review costs, up to RM300,000 per issue.[27]

The subsidy eligibility criteria can encourage the development of a credible market, increasing international investor participation. Aligning eligibility criteria with international 1.5°C-aligned standards will ensure bonds are impactful and meet investor requirements. If eligibility criteria are aligned with those for guarantees and incentives and with any existing climate disclosure requirements, this can minimize the administrative burden of accessing the subsidy.

Subsidy development will likely be simpler than guarantee design, so it could be prioritized to ensure there is support in place in the near term.

---

[25]   ADB. https://www.adb.org/projects/52329–001/main.

[26]   A. Prasad, E. Loukoianova, A. Xiaochen Feng, and W. Oman. 2022. *Mobilizing Private Climate Financing in Emerging Market and Developing Economies*. International Monetary Fund, Staff Climate Notes. https://www.imf.org/en/Publications/staff-climate-notes/Issues/2022/07/26/Mobilizing-Private-Climate-Financing-in-Emerging-Market-and-Developing-Economies-520585.

[27]   Capital Markets Malaysia. 2018. *Incentives – SRI Sukuk and Bond Grant Scheme*. https://www.msfi.com.my/incentives-sri-sukuk-and-bond-grant-scheme/.

Table 3: Examples of Green Financing Instruments

Economy	Green Financing Instrument	Details
People's Republic of China	Green bond subsidies	Implemented in several local governments as part of the People's Bank of China green finance pilot zones.[a]
Hong Kong, China	Green loans	Covers eligible expenses (up to HK$800,000) for borrowers or repeat issuers, and 50% (up to HK$ million) for a first-time issuer.[b]
Singapore	Green and Sustainability-Linked Loan Grant Scheme	Covers the cost of verification, assessment, and up to 60% of the cost of framework development.[c]

Sources:
[a] People's Bank of China. 2019. *PBC Announcement on Supporting the Issuance of Green Debt Financing Instruments by Pilot Zones for Green Finance Reform and Innovations.* http://www.pbc.gov.cn/english/130721/3828774/index.html.
[b] Hong Kong Monetary Authority. *Green and Sustainable Finance Grant Scheme.* https://www.hkma.gov.hk/eng/key-functions/international-financial-centre/bond-market-development/tax-concessions-and-incentive-schemes/.
[c] Monetary Authority of Singapore. 2020. *MAS Launches World's First Grant Scheme to Support Green and Sustainability-Linked Loans.* Press release. 24 November. https://www.mas.gov.sg/news/media-releases/2020/mas-launches-worlds-first-grant-scheme-to-support-green-and-sustainability-linked-loans.

The challenge of developing an ecosystem of subsidies is that there is no guarantee that the presence of subsidies causes the desired change in market behavior. There is a possibility that the presence of the subsidy remains the only reason the targeted market segment prevails. The cost of managing the subsidy and ensuring the right transparency measures are in place can further add to the financial burden of providing subsidies. As such, the provision of a subsidy should be coupled with other efforts to shift investor and issuer long-term priorities for sustainability. In addition, subsidies that historically have led to the risks of market dependency and design should account for the risks of market distortion, which could limit action. Clear communication on phaseout dates can help address these risks.

E.   Sovereign Green, Social, Sustainability, and Sustainability-Linked Bond Issuance

Coordination required: Departments and/or ministries of infrastructure, energy, buildings, transport, environment, agriculture

Some countries in ASEAN+3 have underdeveloped green capital markets. This may be because potential issuers do not see the benefits of issuance and are unsure of demand. Sovereign GSS+ bond issuance demonstrates to the market the visibility and pricing benefits of green bonds and provides guidance to potential local issuers. It also draws international investors to the local market, boosting demand.

Sovereign issuance helps finance a country's net zero pledges. They also demonstrate commitment to climate goals and can help kickstart a local green bond market. If it also achieves a "greenium," due to higher investor demand, then it could provide lower-cost financing for the country than vanilla bond issuance.[28] Germany's green sovereign issuance demonstrates this clearly, as the bonds are twinned with vanilla issuance.[29]

---

[28] The greenium is a new issuer discount when a green bond prices inside the issuer's yield curve in the primary market. Therefore, the issuer obtains cheaper funding for the bond compared to prevailing rates: see C. Harrison. 2023. *Green Bond Pricing in the Primary Market H2 2022.* Climate Bonds Initiative. https://www.climatebonds.net/resources/reports/green-bond-pricing-primary-market-h2-2022.
[29] *Bundesrepublik Deutschland Finanzagentur.* Twin Bond Concept. https://www.deutsche-finanzagentur.de/en/federal-securities/types-of-federal-securities/green-federal-securities/twin-bond-concept.

Sovereign GSS+ bond issuance offers investors a range of sectoral exposures, such as conservation, biodiversity, and adaptation. For example, over 90% of proceeds from Fiji's 2017 green bond were dedicated to adaptation, with Fiji citing climate resilience as its main motivation for issuance.[30]

Multilateral development banks and nongovernment organizations can support sovereign issuance at any or all stages of the process. The World Bank supported the 2018 Seychelles $15 million blue bond with a $5 million partial credit guarantee and a loan to cover the transaction costs. It also introduced the Seychelles to banks, intermediaries, and investors.[31]

Public sector participation will bring confidence to the market. Local currency sovereign issuance can generate demand, providing other issuers with access to low-cost capital. Securing Climate Bonds Certification on sovereign issuance, meanwhile, provides certainty to the market that the bond is Paris-aligned, boosting international investor demand, and will provide best practices on climate ambition to corporate issuers.[32]

Sovereign issuance demonstrates a commitment to net zero. Establishing a regular program of issuance further demonstrates this commitment, with a larger labeled proportion of total debt issuance sending a strong signal of credible commitment.

Several ASEAN+3 countries have issued GSS+ bonds already and could consider issuing them under different labels to promote the breadth of the market.

Sovereign issuance can fund key strategic infrastructure that is needed to facilitate private sector transition investments, such as expansion of the power grid. Investors have highlighted the potential role of sovereign GSS+ issuance in financing sovereign anchor investment in ASEAN power grid connectivity projects. It can also finance the incentives and subsidies outlined above.

When identifying the use of proceeds for the bond issuance, ministries of finance can use green budget tagging, which assesses budget alignment with climate commitments, and may identify a wider pool of eligible expenditure than first expected by the ministry.[33] Tagging can use a national green taxonomy or a global taxonomy, such as the Common Ground Taxonomy developed by the International Platform on Sustainable Finance or Climate Bonds Taxonomy, if a national taxonomy is not in place.

Sovereign issuance and budget tagging processes trigger action within other ministries, as they automatically creates a discipline of assessing spending eligibility, prompting discussions on how to align with the bond framework. This can then lead to real economy policy development that could support the development of a pipeline of issuers.

If the ministry has capacity or expertise gaps, it could contract a third-party consultancy to assist with framework development and expenditure identification. For example, Italy's green bond framework was drafted with support from consultancy group ICF (originally Inner City Fund) and the Climate Bonds Initiative.[34]

---

[30] Government of Fiji. Ministry of Economy. *The Fiji Sovereign Green Bond 2019 Update.* https://www.rbf.gov.fj/wp-content/uploads/2020/03/Fiji-Sovereign-Green-Bond-Impact-Report-2019.pdf.

[31] World Bank. *Seychelles: Introducing the World's First Sovereign Blue Bond - Mobilizing Private Sector Investment to Support the Ocean Economy.* https://pubdocs.worldbank.org/en/242151559930961454/Case-study-Blue-Bond-Seychelles-final-6-7-2019.pdf.

[32] Climate Bonds Initiative. *Certification under the Climate Bonds Standard.* https://www.climatebonds.net/certification.

[33] Ministère de l'Économie, des Finances et de la Souveraineté Industrielle et Numérique. *2020. Budget Vert: La France Est le 1er Pays au Monde à Mesurer L'impact du Budget de l'État sur L'environnement.* https://www.economie.gouv.fr/budget-vert-france-1er-pays-monde-mesurer-impact-budget-etat-environnement.

[34] Government of Italy. Ministry of Economy and Finance. 2021. *The MEF Publishes the Framework for the Issuance of Sovereign Green Bonds.* https://www.mef.gov.it/en/ufficio-stampa/comunicati/2021/The-MEF-publishes-the-Framework-for-the-issuance-of-Sovereign-Green-Bonds-BTP-Green.-Monday-March-1st-at-3.30-p.m-00001.-CET-the-Global-Investor-Call-for-the-Framework-presentation/.

It may be unwise for highly indebted sovereigns to issue more government debt. In such cases, they could restructure existing debt as a sustainability-linked bond, which would provide the same signal benefits of issuance and could possibly secure more favorable interest rates. Some ministries of finance have used debt for nature swaps to reduce their debt-to-gross domestic product ratio while also financing climate and environmental goals.[35] However, such swaps can result in credit rating downgrades, so they are generally only used when the country is in financial distress. Sub-sovereign entities could also be encouraged to issue a GSS+ municipal bond when the sovereign is not able to, or in addition to the sovereign. This can have the same catalytic impacts laid out above; for example, several Chinese municipalities have issued green bonds.[36]

F.   Effectiveness Assessment

Key policies in ASEAN+3 have been mapped, with implementation dates (Table 4).

Of the 10 ASEAN member countries, six have a sustainable finance roadmap in place. Five have also issued a GSS+ sovereign bond, namely Malaysia, Indonesia (by the regulator), Philippines, Singapore, and Thailand.

Table 4: Implementation Date of Key Sustainable Finance Fiscal Policies in the Association of Southeast Asian Nations Plus Three

Policy	Brunei Darussalam	Cambodia	Indonesia	Lao PDR	Malaysia	Myanmar	Philippines	Singapore	Thailand	Viet Nam	PRC	Japan	Korea, Rep. of
Sustainable finance roadmap[a]	–	–	2015 and 2021 (Regulator)	–	2019	–	2021	2019	2021	2021	2022	2023	–
Tax incentives	–	–	2010	–	In force	–	2010	2015	–	–	Subnational	2022	–
Green guarantees	–	–	–	–	2010	–	–	–	–	–	–	–	In force (Korea Credit Guarantee Fund - KODIT)
Green finance subsidies	–	–	2018	–	2017	–	–	In force	–	–	Subnational	In force	Pilot
GSS+ sovereign issuance	–	–	2018	–	2021	–	2022	2022	2020	–	Subnational	Proposed	Pilot

PRC = People's Republic of China; GSS+ = green, social, sustainability, sustainability-linked, and other thematic; Lao PDR = Lao People's Democratic Republic.

Notes: The Association of Southeast Asian Nations Plus Three includes the 10 member states of the Association of Southeast Asian Nations and the PRC, Japan, and the Republic of Korea. Effective 1 February 2021, ADB placed a temporary hold on sovereign project disbursements and new contracts in Myanmar.

[a]   Association of Southeast Asian Nations roadmap introduced in 2023.

Source: Author.

---

[35]   IMF. 2022. Swapping Debt for Climate or Nature Pledges Can Help Fund Resilience. *IMF Blog*. 14 December. https://www.imf.org/en/Blogs/Articles/2022/12/14/swapping-debt-for-climate-or-nature-pledges-can-help-fund-resilience.
[36]   Climate Bonds Initiative and SynTao Green Finance. 2021. *China Green Finance Policy*. https://www.climatebonds.net/files/reports/policy_analysis_report_2021_en_final.pdf.

G.   Impact and Context of Policy Introduction

Nine of the 13 countries have implemented at least one of the fiscal policies. Roadmaps are the most common, including at the ASEAN level, followed by carbon pricing and GSS+ sovereign issuance. Brunei Darussalam, Cambodia, Lao People's Democratic Republic, and Myanmar have not implemented any sustainable finance fiscal policies. They have also not seen any GSS+ issuance, although Cambodia and Myanmar have done some sustainability-linked loan issuance.[37]

Policy introduction and green bond market growth appear to be correlated, with both increasing significantly from 2019.

The GSS+ market in these countries has grown rapidly in recent years, with annual green bond issuance more than doubling in 2019–2021 (Figures 4 and 5). The People's Republic of China accounts for most issuers and issuance volume, but issuance has also grown strongly in ASEAN countries in recent years, driven by Singapore.

Figure 4: Annual Number of Green Bond Issuers, ASEAN+3

Figure 5: Annual Green Bond Issuance, ASEAN+3

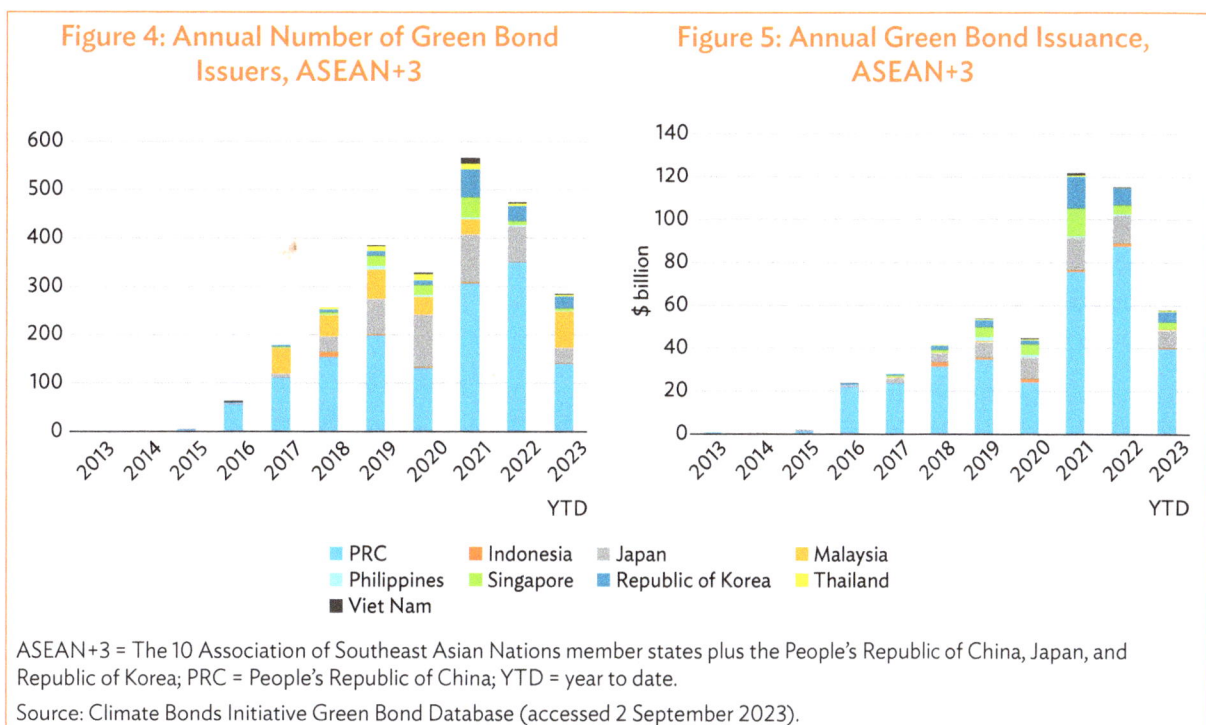

ASEAN+3 = The 10 Association of Southeast Asian Nations member states plus the People's Republic of China, Japan, and Republic of Korea; PRC = People's Republic of China; YTD = year to date.

Source: Climate Bonds Initiative Green Bond Database (accessed 2 September 2023).

ASEAN also has a strongly diversified GSS+ market, with significant social and sustainable bonds and green *sukuk* issuance dominated by sovereigns. Loans also dominate the market, with sustainability-linked and green loans exceeding bond volumes. Policies, therefore, need to target debt issuances in the banking and capital market segments.

---

[37]   M. Almeida and C.X. Wong. 2023. *ASEAN Sustainable Finance State of the Market 2022*. Climate Bonds Initiative. https://www.climatebonds .net/resources/reports/asean-sustainable-finance-state-market-2022. Effective 1 February 2021, ADB placed a temporary hold on sovereign project disbursements and new contracts in Myanmar.

III. Implementation Gaps

To ascertain the impact of these policies, including on sustainable market growth, we have reviewed existing research and engaged with financial market stakeholders in key ASEAN+3 markets.

A.   Barriers Analysis

This report has highlighted key barriers to the growth of sustainable finance markets in ASEAN+3 based on market engagement and desktop research. These barriers may directly limit sustainable issuance, lending, or investment; the government's ability to implement sustainable finance policies; or the efficacy of existing policies.

Primary conclusions from financial market players in ASEAN (Figure 6) identify the top barriers to be the following:

- Pipeline development issues: lack of suitable investments.
- Knowledge and information gaps: lack of technical knowledge.
- Political: regulatory uncertainty.

Figure 6: Greatest Barriers to Sustainable Investment

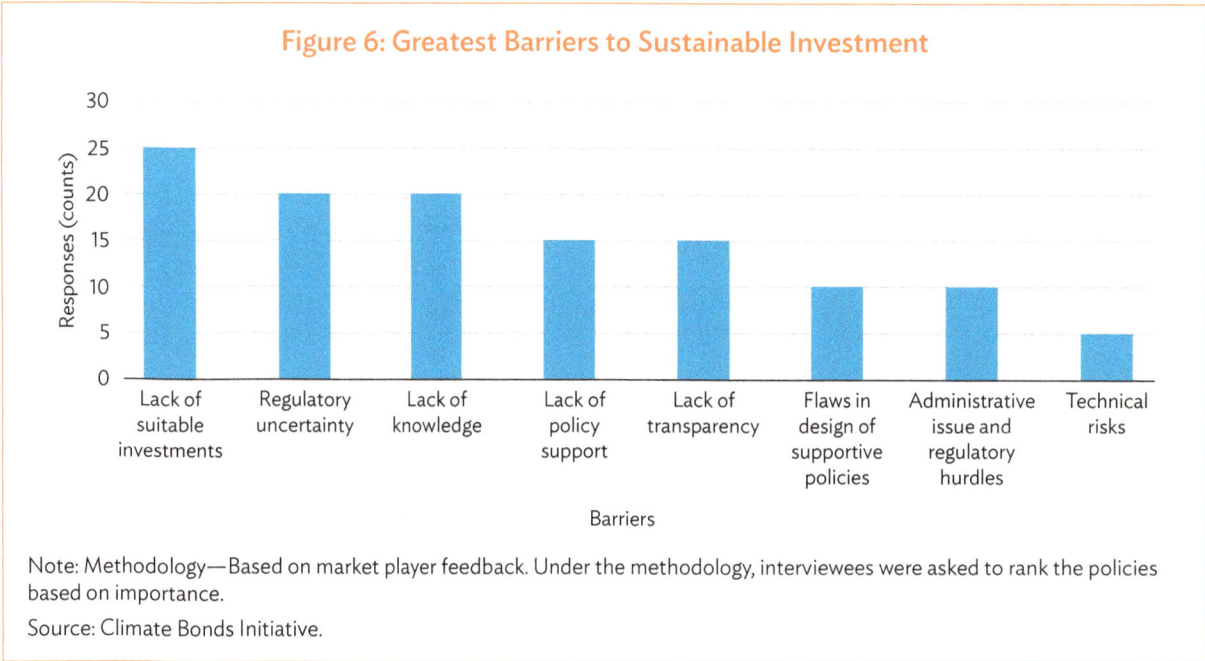

Note: Methodology—Based on market player feedback. Under the methodology, interviewees were asked to rank the policies based on importance.
Source: Climate Bonds Initiative.

Other key barriers are:

- structural, including MSME predominance and currency risks; and
- policy gaps and flaws, including lack of incentives for green and administrative barriers.

1. Knowledge and Information Gaps

- **Need for sustainable investment and project definitions:** Policymakers, issuers, and investors consistently raised the difficulty of identifying sustainable activities. For issuers, it is difficult to identify eligible use of proceeds for GSS+ bonds without a taxonomy, weakening the comprehensiveness of GSS+ bond frameworks.
- **Lack of data and transparency around project-level sustainability and financial performance:**[38] Without climate disclosure requirements for companies, investors find it challenging to evaluate the sustainability of their investments because companies are not obligated to publish full information about their sustainability performance. This exposes them to greenwashing and reputational risks, disincentivizing investment.
- **Underestimation of climate-related financial risks:** Short-term and/or backward-looking risk assessments will naturally underestimate climate-related risks. Transition risks, such as asset stranding, are often underestimated, particularly if there is a lack of policy certainty (see political barriers above). Banks and investors reference a lack of incentive for green investments. This is partly because they do not see the risk in investing in high-carbon assets, in addition to the lack of sufficient "pull factors" for green investments.
- **Elevated risk perception for green projects:** Innovative green technologies may be seen as higher risk as they do not have long track records. They can also be perceived to have uncertain cash flow projections and lower profit margins, particularly climate adaptation projects, constraining their ability to secure financing.[39]
- **Lack of capacity:** Asian asset owners invest only 10% of portfolios in environmental, social, and governance (ESG)-related strategies.[40] The lack of a sustainable project pipeline and the limited issuance of sustainable bonds seems to be partly due to a lack of capacity to identify, manage, and report sustainable investments. Feedback from investors in Singapore and Hong Kong, China, suggests a prevalent information gap and lack of resources and relevant technical capacity between investors and issuers of sustainable assets. These need to be addressed.

2. Pipeline Development Issues

- **Lack of pipeline:** The lack of suitable investments is a key barrier for many ASEAN investors. A 2022 World Bank survey of financial market participants in the ASEAN-5 economies (including banks, asset managers, pension funds, and insurance companies) found the lack of investment opportunities to be one of the top-5 challenges to sustainable investments.[41] Identifiable and/or eligible assets matching financial participants' investment objectives are also lacking. This opinion was held by 50% of respondents in Thailand and 46% in Malaysia.[42]
- **Mismatch between sustainable projects and demand:** Many projects in need of green financing are small-scale and, therefore, reliant on loan financing. Without securitization and aggregation facilities, these are inaccessible to institutional investors.

[38] International Energy Agency. *Cost of Capital Observatory*. https://www.iea.org/reports/cost-of-capital-observatory.
[39] World Bank. 2022. *Unleashing Sustainable Finance in Southeast Asia*. Washington, DC: World Bank. https://openknowledge.worldbank.org/server/api/core/bitstreams/7ff934ad-de0a-5fd0-bed1-42e1de4f5717/content.
[40] Willis Towers Watson. 2021. *Asian Asset Owners: Raising Their ESG Game. ESG Beliefs and Practices Survey 2021: Asia*. https://www.wtwco.com/en-hk/insights/2021/10/asian-asset-owners-raising-their-esg-game.
[41] The ASEAN-5 includes Indonesia, Malaysia, the Philippines, Singapore, and Thailand.
[42] World Bank. 2022. *Unleashing Sustainable Finance in Southeast Asia*. Washington, DC: World Bank. https://openknowledge.worldbank.org/entities/publication/3538d196-f93a-5a7d-b956-19606740a561.

- **Lack of investor or intermediary demand:** Some investors may not see the benefit of investing in sustainable instruments and intermediaries as the benefit of arranging them. This could be due to an underestimation of climate-related risks or short-term investment practices. This is likely best tackled through regulator or central bank action rather than fiscal policy. Financial institutions need to be encouraged to invest/finance in environmentally friendly assets through incentives like lower capital adequacy ratios. The lack of appropriate financing thus impacts companies' efforts to transition to low-emission activities. In addition, cost waivers for bond issuance are now the only direct financial support for sustainable projects.
- **High cost of technical, legal, and financial feasibility studies:** Developing a pipeline of sustainable investments requires significant upfront expenditure on feasibility studies. In some cases, tools for capital investment feasibility studies are limited. These initiation-stage expenditures are also often unsuitable for commercial financing.
- **Additional costs of green, social, sustainability, sustainability-linked, and other thematic issuance:** Compared to loan financing, issuing smaller-sized green bonds is relatively expensive. Some expenses apply to all types of bonds, such as legal fees, obtaining the credit rating, and developing a bond prospectus, while others are exclusive to green bonds, such as obtaining a second-party opinion and green certification. These expenses are minor for larger transactions but might deter smaller transactions.

3. Structural Barriers

- **Micro, small and medium-sized enterprise predominance in the economy:** ASEAN has a very high proportion of MSMEs, contributing 45% of gross domestic product.[43] Such entities are unlikely to tap the capital market and access international sustainable investment flows. Recognizing the importance of the banking sector in this situation, policies, therefore, need to be tailored to this context, e.g., making subsidies available for green loans. In addition, MSMEs may have fewer resources at hand to communicate or collate data attesting to their sustainability and, as such, may not be naturally perceived as a "green investment."
- **Lack of long-term debt financing:** Indonesian banks cannot provide long-term lending due to reliance on short-term deposits.[44] This will particularly constrain renewables projects, which have high upfront costs but low operational costs and so require longer-term financing.
- **Lack of cross-border policy consistency:** Different regulations and definitions in different countries within a region or across multiple regions will make it challenging for investors to invest in multiple regions, and may disincentivize investment in a particular country with distinctly different policy frameworks than regional peers.
- **Currency risks for international investors:** Exchange rates cause fluctuations in investment value and impact the cost of repayment. Local currency issuance, therefore, holds a risk for which international investors often require compensation. A lack of foreign exchange hedging options may limit local currency investment by international investors, and it must be recognized that domestic companies may find hedging tools costly and difficult to arrange should they wish to fundraise in hard currencies.[45]
- **Presence of fossil fuel incumbents:** If the energy market is saturated with fossil fuel generation capabilities, natural demand for expansion of energy sources will be lacking, impacting demand for renewables. Historical demand predictions often led to very high fossil fuel capacity, limiting demand for renewables. For example, in Indonesia, the Philippines, and Viet Nam, electricity generation capacity from fossil fuel-fired power plants

43   ASEAN. 2020. *Development of Micro, Small, and Medium Enterprises in ASEAN (MSME).* The ASEAN Secretariat. Jakarta. https://asean .org/our-communities/economic-community/resilient-and-inclusive-asean/development-of-micro-small-and-medium-enterprises-in-asean-msme/.

44   R. Rakhmadi and M. Sudirman. 2019. *Developing a Guarantee Instrument to Catalyze Renewable Energy Investments in Indonesia.* Climate Policy Initiative. https://climatepolicyinitiative.org/wp-content/uploads/2019/05/Developing-a-Guarantee-Instrument-to-Catalyze-Renewable-Energy-Investments-in-Indonesia.pdf.

45   Climate Bonds Initiative. 2019. *Unlocking Green Bonds in Indonesia: A Guide for Issuers, Regulators and Investors.* https://www.climatebonds .net/files/reports/climate-bonds-indo-barriers-20191219.pdf.

is currently being developed, and existing power capacity, coupled with potential generation from renewable capacity targets, will exceed future electricity demand. This could crowd out renewable energy deployment.[46]

- **Payback periods for some green investments and the maturities of credit options on the market are mismatched.** The World Bank reports that the estimated payback period for energy investments is 3 years for medium firms and 5 years for large firms. However, most credit options available in the market have shorter maturities.[47] For example, Perusahaan Listrik Negara (the Indonesian state-owned electricity company) explores alternatives to finance its planned increase in renewable energy capacity through financing structures such as securitization.

4. Political Sources of Uncertainty

- **Lack of consistency and policy certainty:** Regulatory uncertainty is a major barrier for market players. This increases the riskiness of green investments, increasing the cost of capital. This reduces the efficacy of tax incentives, etc., if they are considered liable to be removed. In addition, investors and policymakers raised the importance of a strong carbon price and the phaseout of fossil fuel subsidies to increase the attractiveness of green investments, with some ranking this as more important than green tax incentives and subsidies.
- **Lack of coordination between government agencies:** Contradictory policies could confuse investors and issuers, for example, if one ministry is more supportive of green development than others. In addition, certain policies may depend on others being in place, such as green subsidy eligibility, which is defined by taxonomy.
- **Lack of mandate from the government:** If climate and sustainability targets are not made a core responsibility for government agencies and regulators, then the above political barriers are more likely to occur. Climate and sustainability targets need to be integrated into development plans to send a clear signal to the market. This is why government-endorsed roadmaps are important, but also that they are based on national climate targets and green development plans.

5. Policy Gaps and Flaws

- **Policies take the form of guidance rather than clear directives.** Investors in two key ASEAN markets commend the intent and foresightedness of their policymakers and regulators in acknowledging the importance of sustainable finance. However, the common feedback is that current announcements and policy issuance are primarily either principles-based or directional papers. While the directional paper is comprehensive and a useful resource for the financial sector, the lack of policy clarity suggests that, for now, frameworks can only serve as a guide to promote sustainable investment. For the policy framework to be effective, concerted efforts are needed to build industry understanding and technical expertise to enable the implementation of sustainable investment across all sectors.
- **Lack of incentives for sustainable investments.** Financial institutions described how they require tax incentives to finance green assets, as based on a traditional risk-return assessment, they may not naturally favor green projects. Primarily, although there is a recognition of long-term transition and physical risk exposure, financial institutions suggest shifting lending criteria now, and some level of encouragement would be needed to invest/finance in environmentally friendly assets through incentives like lower capital adequacy ratios. If financial institutions delay making appropriate financing available, then this will hinder real economy companies from transitioning to low-emission activities. Concessional finance is lacking that could enable private investor participation, particularly for higher-risk projects (due to new technologies, etc.).

---

[46] X. Chen, and D.L. Mauzerall. 2021. The Expanding Coal Power Fleet in Southeast Asia: Implications for Future CO_2 Emissions and Electricity Generation. *Earth's Future*. 9 (12). https://doi.org/10.1029/2021EF002257.

[47] World Bank. 2023. *Indonesia Country Climate and Development Report.* Washington, DC: World Bank. https://www.worldbank.org/en/country/indonesia/publication/indonesia-country-climate-and-development-report.

- **Administrative barriers:** Long permitting processes for infrastructure will limit investment. These barriers often disproportionately limit green investment, as new technologies are more likely to experience regulatory complexity and delayed processing times due to a lack of relevant experience within the public administration. In addition, complex administrative processes for incentive and subsidy schemes could limit uptake —this has been seen in some European countries, as project developers can be confused over eligibility for different schemes.
- **Policies that prevent asset securitization within the banking sector—limiting banks' capacities to lend against assets:** Without securitization, banks are unable to move assets off their balance sheets and cannot increase their lending. This will particularly impact green investments with long payback periods, which require longer-dated lending.[48]
- **Historical policies implemented to support power sector development:** For example, domestic market obligations that prefer coal or pricing that favors dispatchability over availability will put renewable energy developments at a disadvantage. S&P Global Ratings suggests the lower sustainable bond issuance in ASEAN compared to northern Asia could be, in part, due to ASEAN economies' greater dependence on fossil fuels.[49] However, new commitments made by ASEAN countries, such as the Malaysia Renewable Energy Roadmap supporting the decarbonization of the electricity sector through 2035, suggest this situation could be reverted in the future.

---

[48]   World Bank. 2023. *Indonesia Country Climate and Development Report*. Washington, DC. https://www.worldbank.org/en/country/indonesia/publication/indonesia-country-climate-and-development-report.

[49]   Sustainability Insights. 2023. *Asia-Pacific Sustainable Bond Issuance To Increase In 2023*. 14 February. https://www.spglobal.com/_assets/documents/ratings/research/101572592.pdf.

IV. Recommendations

During the consultation with finance sector stakeholders and ASEAN+3 policymakers, respondents ranked our suggested policies highly (Figure 7).

Figure 7: Most Important Policies to Make Sustainable Investment More Attractive to Market Participants

Preference for Fiscal Policy Instruments

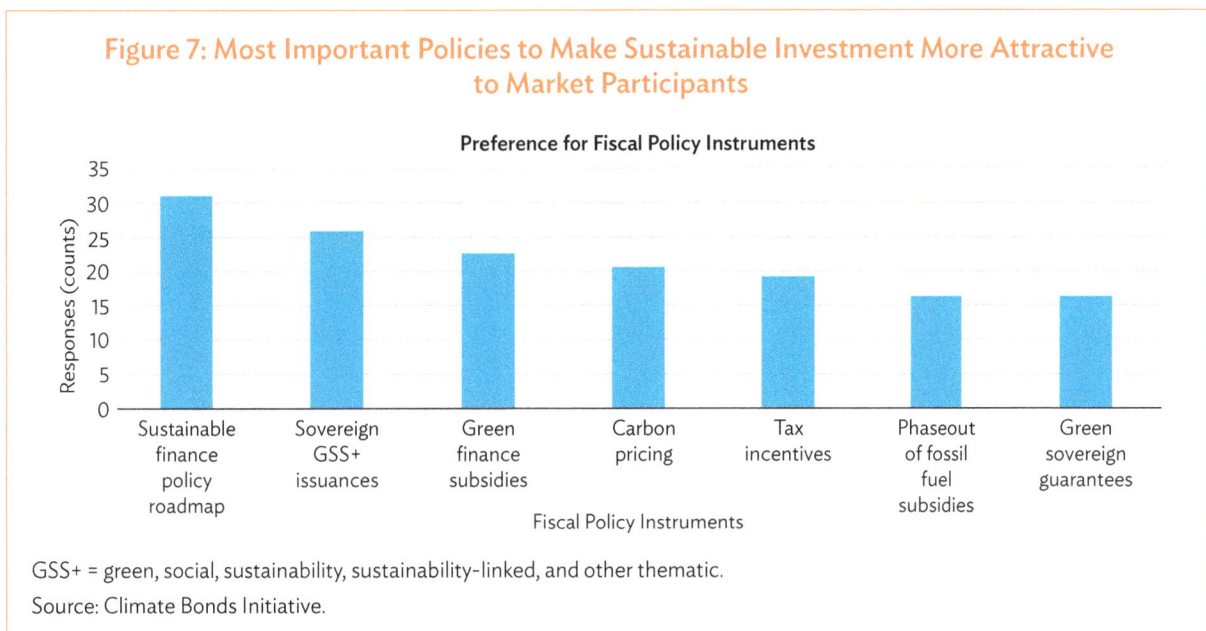

GSS+ = green, social, sustainability, sustainability-linked, and other thematic.
Source: Climate Bonds Initiative.

A. Policy Design Recommendations

Certain design recommendations are applicable to all policies. These will ensure the efficacy of policy implementation. They will address the key barriers of lack of consistency and policy certainty, administrative barriers, and of policies taking the form of guidance rather than clear directives.

- Policymakers should provide confidence that regulations will stay in place in the long term. For example, they could do this by translating net zero targets into legislation that shows a stronger commitment than an announcement of a target and that enables the legal system to address any action that goes against that commitment.[50] In ASEAN, only Brunei Darussalam, Cambodia, Lao People's Democratic Republic, Malaysia, Singapore, and Viet Nam have a 2050 net zero target. This puts the government at risk of litigation if it does

---

[50] Institute for Government. 2020. The Heathrow Judgment is not "Undemocratic Judicial Activism". https://www.instituteforgovernment.org.uk/article/comment/heathrow-judgment-not-undemocratic-judicial-activism.

not meet targets; therefore, it will need to have policies in place that ensure action from other actors that may impact these targets.

- When developing policies, it is important that they reflect the real economy drivers and market players, for example, ensuring that any incentives or guarantees support loans and bonds to reflect a high dependence on loan financing. Malaysia's tax incentive for GSS+ bonds is also available to *sukuk* issued under the Securities Commission Malaysia's SRI *Sukuk* Framework and SRI-linked *Sukuk* Framework, as well as bonds issued under the ASEAN GSS+ Bonds Standards.[51]
- All policies to encourage a shift in behavior should be time-bound, with clear phase-in dates (and potentially phase-out) to provide clarity to the market. For example, the Singapore Exchange (SGX) is introducing mandatory climate reporting in phases from 2022 to 2025.[52]
- Policy design should ensure an efficient administrative burden balanced against the need for transparency and mitigation against possible abuse; for example, clarity on eligibility for guarantees, streamlining subsidy provision, or open-source data to assist climate disclosures.
- Designating a specific policy champion (entity) for each policy can ensure momentum is kept up on introduction and ensures accountability. In addition, this can help when liaising between different ministries or actors (see Mexico Sustainable Finance Committee in Appendix 1).

B.   Policy Recommendations

Figure 8 highlights how the recommended policies address the barriers identified by market players. See section II for description and design recommendations.

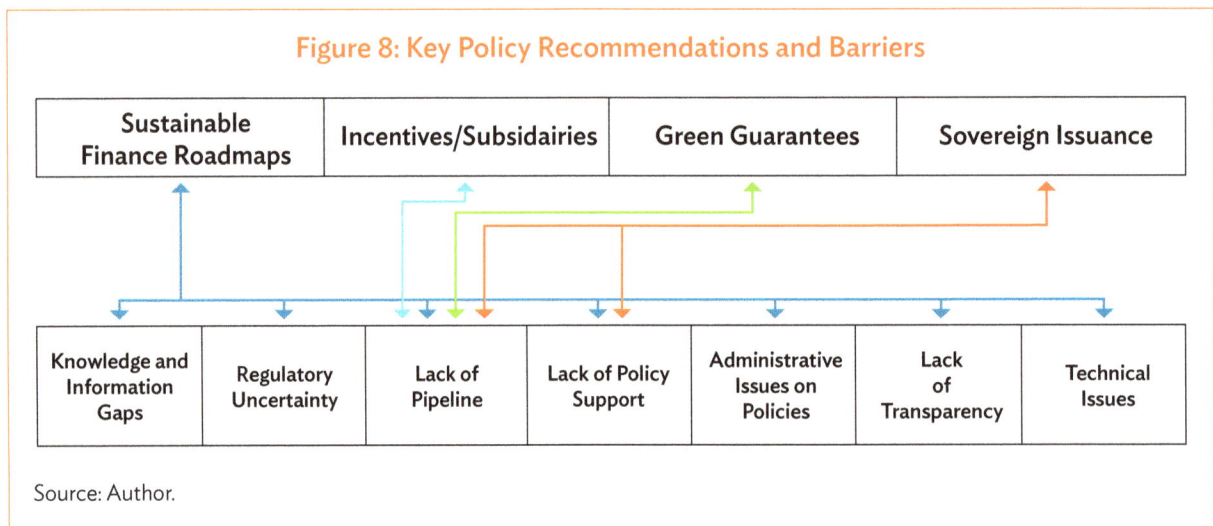

Figure 8: Key Policy Recommendations and Barriers

| Sustainable Finance Roadmaps | Incentives/Subsidairies | Green Guarantees | Sovereign Issuance |

| Knowledge and Information Gaps | Regulatory Uncertainty | Lack of Pipeline | Lack of Policy Support | Administrative Issues on Policies | Lack of Transparency | Technical Issues |

Source: Author.

1. Sustainable Finance Policy Roadmap

- ■ **High priority:** Catalyzing wider policy development.
- ■ **Medium complexity:** Requires multi-stakeholder consultation.

---

[51]   Securities Commission Malaysia. 2022. *Expansion of SRI Sukuk and Bond Grant Scheme to Facilitate Sustainable Finance.* https://www.sc.com.my/resources/media/media-release/expansion-of-sri-sukuk-and-bond-grant-scheme-to-facilitate-sustainable-finance.
[52]   SGX. *Sustainability Reporting.* https://www.sgx.com/sustainable-finance/sustainability-reporting.

- **Barriers addressed:** Lack of investor or intermediary demand, lack of cross-border policy consistency, lack of consistency and policy certainty, lack of coordination between government agencies, lack of government mandate, policies take the form of guidance rather than clear directives.

Case Study

The Government of the Philippines recognizes the importance of mobilizing finance to support sustainable activities and, in 2021, released the Philippine Sustainable Finance Roadmap.[53] The roadmap includes the "strategic action plan in mobilizing finance to support the transition toward a low-carbon and climate-resilient economy," which was developed to support the Philippines' Nationally Determined Contributions to the Paris Agreement.

2. Green Finance Subsidies

- **High priority:** Simpler to implement than guarantees.
- **Low complexity:** Development is less complex than other instruments, particularly if covering the cost of labeled issuance.
- **Barriers addressed:** Elevated risk perception for green projects; high cost of technical, legal, and financial feasibility studies; additional costs of GSS+ issuance.

Case Study

In the ASEAN sustainable debt space, Singapore introduced its Sustainable Bond Grant Scheme in 2017 to encourage GSS+ bond issuance. This was followed in 2021 by the world's first Green and Sustainability-Linked Loan Grant Scheme. The regulator and stock exchange also subsidized fees for green bond issuance and listing.[54]

3. Tax Incentives

- **Medium priority:** Easy to implement.
- **Low complexity:** However, considerations are needed about impacts on the tax base.
- **Barriers addressed:** Elevated risk perception for green projects, lack of investor or intermediary demand, and lack of incentives for sustainable investments.

Case Study

The Government of Malaysia launched the Green Technology Tax Incentive in 2014 to provide the industry with incentives. The Green Investment Tax Allowance is available to companies developing qualifying green technology projects listed under the MyHIJAU Directory for business or own consumption or those purchasing qualifying green technology products.[55]

4. Guarantees for Green and Sustainable Investments

- **Medium priority:** Will de-risk green investments otherwise inaccessible to private investors.
- **High complexity:** Requires evaluation of relevant risks, development of governance mechanisms, assessment of level of coverage and fee structure, and of impact on government balance sheet.
- **Barriers addressed:** Elevated risk perception for green projects, mismatch between sustainable projects and demand, lack of long-term debt financing, and currency risks for international investors.

---

[53] Government of the Philippines. Department of Finance. *The Philippine Sustainable Finance Roadmap.* https://www.dof.gov.ph/wp-content/uploads/2021/10/ALCEP-Roadmap.pdf.

[54] Climate Bonds Initiative. *ASEAN Sustainable Finance State of the Market 2022.* https://www.climatebonds.net/files/reports/cbi_asean_sotm_2022_02f.pdf.

[55] Malaysian Green Technology and Climate Change Centre. *Green Investment Tax Allowance (GITA) & Green Income Tax Exemption (GITE).* https://www.mgtc.gov.my/what-we-do/green-incentives/green-investment-tax-incentives-gita-gite/.

Case Study

In Indonesia, the 2014 47-megawatt Rajamandala hydropower plant project was developed with the support of a $200 million political risk guarantee by the Multilateral Investment Guarantee Agency. This enabled the Japan Bank for International Cooperation and Mizuho Bank to extend a 19-year loan to the project developers. However, in Indonesia, there are no specific green guarantee facilities, meaning that smaller renewables projects are likely to be outcompeted by larger projects.[56]

5. Catalytic Sovereign Issuance

- **High priority:** Able to kickstart private issuance and action among wider government.
- **High complexity:** Requires coordination with multiple departments and other actors.
- **Barriers addressed:** Lack of consistency and policy certainty, lack of government mandate, lack of investor or intermediary demand.

Case Study

Indonesia's green *sukuk* is a sharia-compliant bond with proceeds exclusively for green projects.[57] These projects vary from mitigation measures to resilience activities, and eligibility is outlined in their green *sukuk* framework. The initial investments have kickstarted the green bond market in Indonesia, with wider ASEAN partnerships through the Monetary Authority of Singapore.[58] Over half of investors in green *sukuk* are from outside of ASEAN.[59]

C.   Capacity Building

- **High priority:** Will enable uptake of other policies and catalyze independent action.
- **Low complexity:** Can be contracted from third-party organizations.
- **Barriers addressed:** Lack of capacity, lack of pipeline, elevated risk perception for green projects, lack of investor or intermediary demand.

Targeted capacity building can provide potential issuers and underwriters with the tools to issue GSS+ debt or loans, helping them identify what could qualify for green/sustainable projects and assets or ascertain what needs to be done to make existing assets more sustainable. Capacity building can also significantly address the lack of pipelines, as it raises awareness of the benefits of green issuance.

ASEAN investors also need capacity building, given limited ESG investment strategies among them. During consultation, policymakers highlighted the importance of staff capacity and knowledge in processes such as GSS+ sovereign bond expenditure identification (see II.E. Sovereign Green, Social, Sustainability, and Sustainability-Linked Bond Issuance).

If the government has issued sovereign GSS+ debt, it can share these experiences in capacity building and can provide guidance on pricing and deal size. This can also provide potential issuers with confidence in demand for labeled local currency debt. This was a significant motivation for the Government of Thailand when it issued its first Sustainability Bond in 2020 to provide guidance to private market players to grow sustainable debt markets.

56   Climate Policy Initiative. 2019. *Developing a Guarantee Instrument to Catalyze Renewable Energy Investments in Indonesia.* https://www. climatepolicyinitiative.org/publication/developing-a-guarantee-instrument-to-catalyze-renewable-energy-investments-in-indonesia/.

57   United Nations Development Programme. *Indonesia's Green Sukuk Initiative.* INS-UNDP-Indonesia-Sustainable-Development-Financing.pdf.

58   Philippe H. Le Houérou. 2018. A Catalyst for Green Financing in Indonesia. *World Bank Blogs.* 2 August. https://blogs.worldbank.org/ eastasiapacific/catalyst-green-financing-indonesia.

59   Government of Indonesia. Ministry of Finance. *GREEN SUKUK Allocation and Impact Report 2023.* https://api-djppr.kemenkeu.go.id/web/api/ v1/media/C65110FE-4CAF-4C08-9DF7-E3FEFA1BB61B.

In addition to green definitions, capacity building should focus on enhancing knowledge of innovative financing structures and related support, such as guarantees, subsidies, and incentive availability. This includes those provided by third parties, such as development banks, as they are experienced in other markets. This can influence policymakers and ensure the uptake of these support schemes when and if implemented.

Case Study

The 2019 ASEAN Catalytic Green Finance Facility aims to increase green infrastructure investments in Southeast Asia and provides ASEAN member governments with technical assistance. The facility provides knowledge and training programs to strengthen the regulatory environment and build government institutional capacity to scale up green infrastructure investments. It also provides access to over $1 billion in loans.[60]

Malaysia's capital market regulator, Securities Commission Malaysia, via its affiliate Capital Markets Malaysia, set up three Centers of Excellence: one for investors, one for intermediaries, and another for issuers and corporates. The centers provide a regular training schedule, sharing of international best practices, workshops, study tours to more advanced financial markets, and so on. The centers were set up in 2020 as a recommendation of the Malaysian Green Financing Task Force to ascertain market barriers limiting the availability of finance for renewable energy projects.

A challenge certain markets face in the provision of capacity building is that although the initial burden of providing training, market awareness, and technical guidance is at the cost of the government, the program should be developed in such a manner that the financial sector players also contribute to the costs of capacity building to ensure commitment.

It is important to acknowledge that although there are many programs in place in ASEAN to support policymakers and financial market players in understanding sustainable finance, the necessary changes in behavior, priorities, and investment and funding decisions have not been significantly made. Sustainable finance is still a new concept, and it is believed that an effective approach would be to implement capacity building alongside strong regulations that require compliance within a certain time frame.

D. Non-Fiscal Policies Crucial to the Success of Sustainable Fiscal Policies

The success of the policies above depends on the implementation of wider supportive policies, particularly by the central bank and regulators. These will often be included in sustainable finance policy roadmaps.

1. Taxonomy

- **High priority:** Provides clarity on credible investments and can form the basis of eligibility criteria in other policies.
- **Medium complexity:** Developers can use existing regional and global taxonomies to expedite development.
- **Barriers addressed:** Need for green definitions and policies to take the form of guidance rather than clear directives.

---

[60]   ASEAN Catalytic Green Finance Facility. What We Do. ADB. https://www.adb.org/what-we-do/funds/asean-catalytic-green-finance -facility/overview.

Developing a taxonomy is crucial to building a strong and credible sustainable finance market. While the regional ASEAN Taxonomy is in place, a national taxonomy is very important that is aligned with the regional taxonomy but tailored to the national context. A taxonomy identifies investments, assets, and activities that deliver certain sustainability objectives. They aim to improve transparency for investors, encourage financing of activities that reduce greenhouse gas emissions and ecological degradation, and inform financial supervision. They can guide project development, helping grow a pipeline of credible green projects.

Including objectives such as biodiversity in the taxonomy increases the scope of investments that can be included and ensures that these environmental objectives are not excluded from sustainable financing. These could draw on the International Finance Corporation Biodiversity Finance Reference Guide.[61]

For the taxonomy to build a credible sustainable finance market, criteria should be clear, science-based, and aligned with global and local standards. Global alignment will prevent market fragmentation and enable international investment, which is particularly important for countries without a strong local investment base.[62] It will also reduce the burden for international investors aligning with several different taxonomies.

Taxonomy developers can use the International Platform on Sustainable Finance's Common Ground Taxonomy as a starting point in taxonomy development. For example, Hong Kong, China has adopted the Common Ground Taxonomy to facilitate international collaboration and to act as a hub for capital flows.[63]

Although taxonomies address the lack of clarity as to what constitutes an environmentally sustainable activity, there is a potential risk of fragmentation, which could be exacerbated if countries develop such taxonomies without coordination. Divergent classifications can create inconsistency, making it challenging for investors to identify what can be categorized as a sustainable activity.

Case Study

Malaysia's capital market regulator, Securities Commission Malaysia, launched its sustainable and responsible investment (SRI) taxonomy in 2022.[64] The taxonomy is built around four environmental objectives (mitigation, adaptation, biodiversity, and circular economy) and three social objectives (conduct towards consumers and end-users, towards workers, and towards affected communities and wider society), alongside a sustainability component that encourages the alignment to government considerations in addition to the environmental and social objectives.[65] Through these components, the SRI Taxonomy provides guidance to capital market intermediaries, issuers, and investors on the definition and classification of economic activities vis-à-vis sustainable investment.

The SRI taxonomy is designed to be interoperable and consistent with the ASEAN Taxonomy for Sustainable Finance (Version 1) and the Malaysian central bank's climate change taxonomy but specific to Malaysia's stage of economic development and sustainability journey.

[61]   International Finance Corp. 2020. *Biodiversity Finance Reference Guide.* https://www.ifc.org/content/dam/ifc/doc/mgrt/biodiversity-finance-reference-guide.pdf.

[62]   Climate Bonds Initiative. *Global Green Taxonomy Development, Alignment, and Implementation.* https://www.climatebonds.net/files/reports/cbi_taxonomy_ukpact_2022_eng.pdf.

[63]   M. Deng and M. MacGeoch. 2022. *Hong Kong Green and Sustainable Debt Market Briefing 2021.* Climate Bonds Initiative. https://www.climatebonds.net/resources/reports/hong-kong-green-and-sustainable-debt-market-briefing-2021.

[64]   Securities Commission Malaysia. 2022. *SC Unveils Principles-Based Sustainable and Responsible Investment Taxonomy for the Malaysian Capital Market.* Kuala Lumpur. https://www.sc.com.my/resources/media/media-release/sc-unveils-principles-based-sustainable-and-responsible-investment-taxonomy-for-the-malaysian-capital-market.

[65]   Securities Commission Malaysia. 2022. *Principles-based Sustainable and Responsible Investment Taxonomy for the Malaysian Capital Market.* Kuala Lumpur.

2. Regulatory Requirements

- **Medium priority:** Will ensure action from all regulated entities, regardless of the level of interest in sustainable investment.
- **Low complexity:** May require capacity building to enable compliance.
- **Barriers addressed:** Lack of data and transparency around project-level sustainability and financial performance, and policies take the form of guidance rather than clear directives.

Regulation is key to efficiently shifting investment to become more net zero-aligned. These include climate disclosure requirements, incorporating climate responsibility into senior leadership responsibility, and central bank green capital and reserve requirements.[66] The regulation also does not involve direct expenditure in the same way that incentives and subsidies do, so it is likely to be a lower-cost way of encouraging change.

In particular, mandatory transition plan disclosure requirements would encourage the whole economy transition, fostering a transition strategy within reporting entities, providing investors and lenders with the information to assess risks, and supporting policymakers and regulators to understand the economy's exposure to climate risks and net zero trajectories.[67] The proposed regulatory mechanism would cover financial institutions and companies and could be introduced via a staggered approach, focusing on larger institutions, highly polluting, and/or hard-to-abate sectors first.

Climate Bonds Initiative and others have provided important guidance on decarbonization pathways and what should be included in transition plan disclosure. For instance, mandatory transition plan disclosure is included in UK and EU disclosure requirements. The UK Transition Plan Taskforce's Disclosure Framework provides a detailed standard for good practice transition planning, aligned with the International Sustainability Standards Board disclosure standards (footnote 67). These guides can be adapted to the local context to provide local actors with granular guidance on how to develop robust transition plans.

Climate disclosures and transition plan disclosures can also inform the preferential treatment of assets and eligibility for subsidies. For example, the European Central Bank now tilts its corporate bond purchase based on issuer-specific climate scores, partially based on the ambition of climate targets.[68]

Introducing climate disclosure requirements increases the reporting burden on corporations. Providing capacity building and guidance can help ease this while also ensuring that disclosures are useful for decision-making.

Case Study

The Monetary Authority of Singapore has announced that it will set supervisory expectations for financial institutions' transition planning. It will provide guidance on transition planning, covering financial institutions' governance frameworks and client engagement processes. This will enable them to manage climate-related financial risks and to finance real economy transition.[69]

---

[66] L. Burge. 2023. *101 Sustainable Finance Policies for 1.5°C*. Climate Bonds Initiative. https://www.climatebonds.net/resources/reports/101-sustainable-finance-policies-15%C2%B0c-0.

[67] UK Transition Plan Taskforce. 2023. *Disclosure Framework*. https://transitiontaskforce.net/disclosure-framework/.

[68] European Central Bank. 2022. ECB Provides Details on How It Aims to Decarbonise Its Corporate Bond Holdings. News release. 19 September. https://www.ecb.europa.eu/press/pr/date/2022/html/ecb.pr220919~fae53c59bd.en.html.

[69] Monetary Authority of Singapore. 2023. MAS to Set Expectations on Credible Transition Planning by Financial Institutions. News release. 8 June. https://www.mas.gov.sg/news/media-releases/2023/mas-to-set-expectations-on-credible-transition-planning-by-financial-institutions.

3. Real Economy Policies

- ■ **Medium priority:** Will grow a pipeline of sustainable investments.
- ■ **Medium to low complexity:** Most priorities will not require significant cross-government coordination.
- ■ **Barriers addressed:** Lack of pipeline, presence of fossil fuel incumbents, historical policies implemented to support power sector development.

Respondents raised the importance of real economy policy in supporting sustainable finance growth, citing the United States Inflation Reduction Act, which provides long-term tax incentives for renewables development.[70]

Long-term offtake agreements can help de-risk investments beyond guarantee provision. Long-term power purchase agreements and transparent auction processes for renewable electricity can increase certainty for renewables investments. Auctions are one of the most effective policies in boosting renewables investment in emerging markets but are present in only 50% of these markets.[71]

Including real economy policies in sustainable finance policies and roadmaps will also reduce overall government costs. For example, mandates on phaseout or the use of certain technologies are likely to be less expensive than providing subsidies for green.

Subsidies to support investment in low-carbon energy and innovative technologies help bring down the cost curve for nascent clean solutions and accelerate their uptake. However, subsidies should also be gradually reduced to the point where such technologies become competitive with conventional ones.

A lack of financial room can hamper the implementation of policies that directly affect the economy in situations where there is restricted flexibility in government budgets. This issue can be resolved by introducing environmental tax reforms which will discourage activities that damage the environment while also generating revenues for public investment.[72] To address other potential risks related to the implementation of real economy policies, a strong governance system and well-targeted subsidies are also necessary.

Case Study

Indonesia has successfully introduced incentives to develop its electric vehicle battery industry, using its natural advantage as a significant source of nickel. By building the batteries in the country rather than exporting the raw minerals, the country has captured more of the value in the supply chain, and these policies have encouraged foreign companies such as Hyundai and LG to base their factories there. New policies are being developed to build electric vehicles in the country, attracting other international companies, such as Ford and Tesla.[73] These incentives have accelerated the pipeline for renewable energy infrastructure and simultaneously moved Indonesia up the value chain in the clean energy transition.[74]

[70] United States 117th Congress (2021–2022). 2022. *Inflation Reduction Act of 2022*, H.R.5376, https://www.congress.gov/bill/117th-congress/house-bill/5376.

[71] BloombergNEF. 2021. *ClimateScope 2021*. https://global-climatescope.org/downloads/climatescope-2021-report.pdf.

[72] L. Burge. 2023. *101 Sustainable Finance Policies for 1.5°C*. Climate Bonds Initiative. https://www.climatebonds.net/files/reports/cbi_101_policyideas.pdf.

[73] G. Suroyo, K. Lamb, and A. Teresia. 2023. *Exclusive: President Jokowi "Confident" Tesla Will Invest in Indonesia. Reuters.* 1 February. https://www.reuters.com/business/autos-transportation/president-jokowi-confident-tesla-will-invest-indonesia-2023-02-01/.

[74] Australian National University. 2023. *Linking Economic Nationalism with Global Value Chain Indonesia's Nickel Sector Industrial Policies.* https://static1.squarespace.com/static/6073e7bd03c5b9274751137e/t/641b8a95f6a6cd759b2c6558/1679526555839/Linking+economic+nationalism+with+global+value+chain.pdf.

4. Enhance National Development Bank Capacity

- **Medium priority:** Will grow a pipeline of sustainable investments and target MSMEs.
- **Medium to low complexity:** Development banks are already increasing green financing.
- **Barriers addressed:** Lack of pipeline, mismatch between sustainable projects and demand, MSME predominance in the economy, mismatch of payback periods for some green investments, and the maturities of credit options on the market.

National development banks (also described as public banks), national development finance institutions, policy banks, or promotional banks, are fully or partially government-owned financial institutions with an explicit mandate to achieve certain socioeconomic goals in a region or sector.

Several natural characteristics of national development banks enable them to perform a pivotal role in sustainable domestic development. Their domestic mandate and subsequent experience of domestic needs and barriers to finance provide the banks a competitive advantage to shift the real economy to sustainability. They primarily deal in local currency and, given their size, can design innovative and tailored financing structures to meet a country's needs. For example, in infrastructure projects, they can provide grants for the riskiest preconstruction phase and, subsequently, guarantees, debt, and/or equity during construction and operations.

For national development banks to be effective "green banks," governments need to provide direction and mandates to these domestic banks to be more sustainable and reprioritize their lending criteria. At a minimum, they should not be investing in fossil fuel expansion. A robust sustainability strategy will enable them to meet both climate and social priorities. The European Investment Bank provides an example, setting out a Climate Bank Roadmap, targeting 50% sustainable lending by 2025 and for all lending to do no significant harm to the Paris Agreement goals.[75] Governments can also establish green investment quotas for the development bank and encourage them to focus on mobilizing private capital, possibly by setting crowding in targets.

Beyond greening their lending, development banks can unlock huge levels of capital by focusing on crowding in private capital. Rather than investing in 100% of a project, they can provide anchor investment, guarantees, or concessional blended finance for sustainable projects. This can de-risk them enough to attract private investment into the project. This means the project takes up less of the balance sheet, enabling them to finance more. The balance sheet can also be freed up by not holding investments to maturity but instead selling them once the project is past the initiation phase—following a commercial banking model.

Guarantees hold a liability risk and require sufficient balance sheet capacity to ensure the bank's ability to fulfill the guarantee if called upon. Robust monitoring mechanisms can ensure that guarantees and other blending mechanisms do not exceed balance sheet liquidity.[76]

Development banks are significant financiers for MSMEs. By greening their lending criteria and providing capacity building to MSMEs on green project development, they could tilt a significant portion of the economy to green— MSMEs contribute 45% of ASEAN gross domestic product. For example, the Business Development Bank of Canada's mandate is to provide small enterprises support to shift to become prosperous, inclusive, and green.

---

75   European Investment Bank. 2020. *EIB Group Climate Bank Roadmap 2021–2025*. Luxembourg: EIB. https://www.eib.org/attachments/thematic/eib_group_climate_bank_roadmap_en.pdf.

76   Prasad, A., E. Loukoianova, A. Xiaochen Feng, W. Oman. 2022. *Mobilizing Private Climate Financing in Emerging Market and Developing Economies*. IMF Staff Climate Notes. Washington, DC. https://www.imf.org/en/Publications/staff-climate-notes/Issues/2022/07/26/Mobilizing-Private-Climate-Financing-in-Emerging-Market-and-Developing-Economies-520585.

There is a risk of resistance from the development bank if they see green lending requirements as competing with social priorities. Therefore, it is important to highlight the social benefits of climate investments. Development banks could also be encouraged to increase finance for adaptation and resilience due to the strong alignment with social priorities. This is also a major financing gap, receiving only 35% of climate finance flows.[77]

Lastly, it has been debated whether the establishment of a dedicated new green bank would be more effective than shifting the priorities and mandates of existing national development banks. There have been attempts to do so, but the results were not as envisaged for several reasons. It must be recognized that existing national development banks have an established infrastructure, network, relationship, and reach to the nation. The cost of recreating this infrastructure would be prohibitive and time-consuming. More importantly, understanding the client base, the credit profile, and the priorities of real economy players is an intangible asset that takes time to develop and deepen. As such, shifting the mandate and priorities of existing players is more effective.

Case Study

Thailand's state-owned EXIM bank issued small and medium-sized enterprise-focused green bonds in 2022 and 2023, with a fixed maturity period of 3 years.[78] These are use-of-proceeds bonds, with small businesses associated with the "bio-circular-green" economy eligible for them. In particular, the money has been used to support clean energy in industrial applications and its production. Nearly $100 million was issued in the initial offering; oversubscription was 2.5 times the offering. To be attractive to small borrowers, the bonds have low, stable interest rates with semi-regular payback periods.

---

[77]   European Investment Bank. 2022. *2021 Joint Report on Multilateral Development Banks' Climate Finance.* https://www.eib.org/en/publications/ 2021-joint-report-on-multilateral-development-banks-climate-finance.

[78]   https://thainews.prd.go.th/en/news/detail/TCATG230607114605705.

V. Conclusions

A single policy cannot address prevalent market barriers to sustainable investments—an effective strategy instead would create a holistic landscape of policies, initiatives, and government support. This paper recommends starting with a sustainable finance roadmap and then recommends policies that can form a strong foundation for the start of this journey and be easily designed and implemented simultaneously.

By considering the country's specific barriers to sustainable investment and financial market characteristics, ministries of finance will be able to develop robust and fiscally efficient policy packages that can rapidly scale sustainable investment flows.

More importantly, ministries of finance can lead by contributing and supporting climate change priorities in other ministries. The financial market is merely an intermediary that facilitates the funding of real economic activities. As such, fiscal policies should support real economy policies by aligning ambition and priorities.

Ministries of finance can trigger such policy reactions through targeted interventions, as they naturally create a domino effect within the government machinery. Prioritizing climate mitigation and adaptation in fiscal policy, budgeting, public procurement, and investment management strongly signals policy priorities. They are the center of government and can drive change through their impact on economic strategy and fiscal policies.

APPENDIX 1
Global Policy Examples

Mexico Sustainable Finance Committee

Established in 2020 as part of the Financial Stability Council, the committee is the lead agency for sustainable finance, with five working groups, each led by a financial authority: Sustainable Finance Taxonomy; Capital Mobilization Opportunities; Environmental, Social, and Governance Risk Measurement; Disclosure of Information and Adoption of Environmental, Social, and Governance Standards; and implementation of the International Sustainability Standards Board's standards.[1] This exemplifies how strong institutional capacity can ensure a specific champion for every policy.

---

[1]   Network for Green the Financial System. 2022. *In Conversation with Rafael del Villar Alrich.* https://www.ngfs.net/sites/default/files/medias/documents/in-conversation-with-banco-de-mexico.pdf.

APPENDIX 2
List of Stakeholders Interviewed and Questionnaires

- Three departments and/or ministries of finance
- Four investors (in Singapore, Thailand, Viet Nam)
- Three issuers (in Malaysia, Thailand, Viet Nam)

Questionnaires

A.   Ministry of Finance

1.   Which sectors do you regulate or formulate policies on?
2.   Do you have a specific sustainability or climate objective/mandate?
3.   What is your primary objective in supporting sustainable finance?

- Support national climate targets
- Ensure economic growth
- Reduce the country's exposure to financial risks
- Align with international standards (e.g., Task Force on Climate-Related Financial Disclosures)
- Other

Please consider the following policies and indicate which is most important to encourage sustainable investment (score each option 1–5, where 1 is not important, 5 is very important).

- Sustainable finance policy roadmap
- Phaseout of fossil fuel subsidies
- Carbon pricing
- Tax incentives
- Green sovereign guarantees
- Green finance subsidies
- Sovereign green, social, sustainability, and sustainability-linked bond issuance

4.   How effective is the country's policy framework in encouraging and enabling sustainable investment? (If relevant, provide examples.)
5.   What are the key barriers to sustainable investment in this country? (select top-3 most impactful barriers.)

- Lack of suitable investments – size, sector, level of ambition, credit quality
- Regulatory uncertainty
- Lack of policy support
- Flaws in the design of supportive policies
- Administrative issues and regulatory hurdles

- Lack of transparency – reporting, framework, agreed definitions
- Lack of knowledge (technical, opportunities)
- Technical Risks

6. What are the barriers (if any) limiting your ability to implement sustainable finance policies?

- Lack of mandate/uncertainty if within remit
- Political priorities
- Short-term thinking vs. long-term climate goals
- Lack of capacity/technical knowledge
- Other

7. Are there other countries where you have identified a best practice or particularly interesting policy measure/funding scheme that would benefit this country?

B. Investors

1. Which ASEAN country/ies do you invest in?
2. What sectors do you invest in?
3. Do you have a specific sustainable investment mandate?
4. What percentage of your assets under management is currently invested in sustainable investment, and within that, what is the asset class split?
5. About your interest in sustainable finance - What is the primary objective?

- To reduce exposure to financial risk for organizations you represent/supervise
- To re-orientate investment in response to environmental, social, and governance concerns
- To respond to the public interest and enhance your reputation
- Reporting requirements, e.g., organizations' environmental, social, and governance reporting
- Anticipation of future performance
- Other

6. Please consider the following policies and indicate which could/do make investing in sustainable investment products more attractive (score each option 1-5, where 1 is not important, 5 is very important).

- Sustainable finance policy roadmap
- Phaseout of fossil fuel subsidies
- Carbon pricing
- Tax incentives
- Green sovereign guarantees
- Green finance subsidies
- Sovereign green, social, sustainability, and sustainability-linked bond issuance

7. How effective is the country's policy framework in encouraging and enabling sustainable investment? (If relevant, provide examples).

8. What are the key barriers to sustainable investment in this country? Select the top 3 most impactful barriers.

    •   Lack of suitable investments—size, sector, level of ambition, credit quality
    •   Regulatory uncertainty
    •   Lack of policy support
    •   Flaws in the design of supportive policies
    •   Administrative issues and regulatory hurdles
    •   Lack of transparency – reporting, framework, agreed definitions
    •   Lack of knowledge (technical, opportunities)
    •   Technical risks

9. Are there other countries where you have identified a best practice or particularly interesting policy measure/funding scheme that would benefit this country?

C. Issuers

1. Which ASEAN country/ies do you issue/borrow in?
2. What sectors do you issue/borrow in?
3. Do you have a net zero or other emissions target?
4. Please consider the following policies and indicate which could/do make issuing a sustainable investment product more attractive (score each option 1-5, where 1 is not important, 5 is very important).

    •   Sustainable finance policy roadmap
    •   Phaseout of fossil fuel subsidies
    •   Carbon pricing
    •   Tax incentives
    •   Green sovereign guarantees
    •   Green finance subsidies
    •   Sovereign green, social, sustainability, and sustainability-linked bond issuance

5. How effective is the country's policy framework in encouraging and enabling sustainable investment? (If relevant, provide examples).

6. What are the key barriers to sustainable investment in this country? (select the top 3 most impactful barriers).

    •   Lack of suitable investments—size, sector, level of ambition, credit quality
    •   Regulatory uncertainty
    •   Lack of policy support
    •   Flaws in the design of supportive policies
    •   Administrative issues and regulatory hurdles
    •   Lack of transparency – reporting, framework, agreed definitions
    •   Lack of knowledge (technical, opportunities)
    •   Technical risks

7. Are there other countries where you have identified a best practice or particularly interesting policy measure/funding scheme that would benefit this country?

References

A. Prasad, E. Loukoianova, A. Xiaochen Feng, and W. Oman. 2022. *Mobilizing Private Climate Financing in Emerging Market and Developing Economies*. International Monetary Fund, Staff Climate Notes. https://www.imf.org/en/Publications/staff-climate-notes/Issues/2022/07/26/Mobilizing-Private-Climate-Financing-in-Emerging-Market-and-Developing-Economies-520585.

Australian National University. 2023. Linking Economic Nationalism with Global Value Chain Indonesia's Nickel Sector Industrial Policies.

B. Buhr, U. Volz, C. Donovan, G. Kling, Y.C. Lo, V. Murinde, and N. Pullin. 2018. Climate Change and the Cost of Capital in Developing Countries. UN Environment. https://eprints.soas.ac.uk/26038.

BloombergNEF. 2021. *ClimateScope 2021*.

Capital Markets Malaysia. 2018. Incentives – SRI Sukuk and Bond Grant Scheme. https://www.msfi.com.my/incentives-sri-sukuk-and-bond-grant-scheme/.

Climate Bonds Initiative. 2022. ASEAN Sustainable Finance State of the Market 2022. https://www.climatebonds.net/files/reports/cbi_asean_sotm_2022_02f.pdf.

Climate Bonds Initiative. 2019. Unlocking Green Bonds in Indonesia: A Guide for Issuers, Regulators and Investors.

Climate Bonds Initiative. 2023. *101 Sustainable Finance Policies for 1.5°C*. https://www.climatebonds.net/resources/reports/101-sustainable-finance-policies-15%C2%B0c-0.

Climate Bonds Initiative and SynTao Green Finance. 2021. China Green Finance Policy. https://www.climatebonds.net/files/reports/policy_analysis_report_2021_en_final.pdf.

Climate Policy Initiative. 2021. Global Landscape of Climate Finance 2021. https://www.climatepolicyinitiative.org/publication/global-landscape-of-climate-finance-2021/.

Climate Policy Initiative. 2019. Developing a Guarantee Instrument to Catalyze Renewable Energy Investments in Indonesia. https://www.climatepolicyinitiative.org/publication/developing-a-guarantee-instrument-to-catalyze-renewable-energy-investments-in-indonesia/.

Coalition of Finance Ministers for Climate Action and UNDP Financial Centers for Sustainability. 2021. *An Analysis of Sustainable Finance Roadmaps*. https://www.financeministersforclimate.org/news/hp5-publishes-sustainable-finance-roadmaps-report.

European Central Bank. 2022. ECB Provides Details on How It Aims to Decarbonise Its Corporate Bond Holdings. News release. 19 September. https://www.ecb.europa.eu/press/pr/date/2022/html/ecb .pr220919~fae53c59bd.en.html.

European Commission. 2018. Renewed Sustainable Finance Strategy and Implementation of the Action Plan on Financing Sustainable Growth. https://ec.europa.eu/info/publications/sustainable-finance-renewed-strategy_en.

European Investment Bank. 2022. 2021 Joint Report on Multilateral Development Banks' Climate Finance.

European Investment Bank. 2020. *EIB Group Climate Bank Roadmap 2021–2025*. Luxembourg: EIB.

Finance Ministers for Climate. 2023. Strengthening the Role of Ministries of Finance in Driving Climate Action. https://www.financeministersforclimate.org/sites/cape/files/inline-files/Summary%20Strengthening%20 the%20Role%20of%20Finance%20Ministries.pdf.

Fitch Ratings. 2021. Special Report: Climate Change "Stranded Assets" Area Long-Term Risk for Some Sovereigns. https://www.fitchratings.com/research/sovereigns/climate-change-strandedassets-are-long -term-risk-for-some-sovereigns-15–02–2021.

G. Suroyo, K. Lamb, and A. Teresia. 2023. Exclusive: President Jokowi "Confident" Tesla Will Invest in Indonesia. *Reuters*. 1 February. https://www.reuters.com/business/autos-transportation/president-jokowi-confident-tesla-will-invest-indonesia-2023-02-01/.

Government of the United Kingdom. 2021. Greening Finance: A Roadmap to Sustainable Investing. https://www.gov.uk/government/publications/greening-finance-a-roadmap-to-sustainable-investing.

ICMA. n.d. Bond Market Size. https://www.icmagroup.org/market-practice-and-regulatory-policy/secondary -markets/bond-market-size/.

IMF. 2022. Swapping Debt for Climate or Nature Pledges Can Help Fund Resilience. *IMF Blog*. 14 December. https://www.imf.org/en/Blogs/Articles/2022/12/14/swapping-debt-for-climate-or-nature-pledges-can-help-fund-resilience.

Institute for Government. 2020. The Heathrow Judgment is not "Undemocratic Judicial Activism". https://www.instituteforgovernment.org.uk/article/comment/heathrow-judgment-not-undemocratic -judicial-activism.

Intergovernmental Panel on Climate Change. 2021. Climate Change 2021: The Physical Science Basis. Contribution of Working Group I to the Sixth Assessment Report of the Intergovernmental Panel on Climate Change.

International Finance Corp. 2020. *Biodiversity Finance Reference Guide.*

L. Burge. 2023. *101 Sustainable Finance Policies for 1.5°C*. Climate Bonds Initiative. https://www.climatebonds.net/ resources/reports/101-sustainable-finance-policies-15%C2%B0c-0.

M. Almeida and C.X. Wong. 2023. *ASEAN Sustainable Finance State of the Market 2022*. Climate Bonds Initiative. https://www.climatebonds.net/resources/reports/asean-sustainable-finance-state-market-2022.

M. Deng and M. MacGeoch. 2022. *Hong Kong Green and Sustainable Debt Market Briefing 2021*. Climate Bonds Initiative. https://www.climatebonds.net/resources/reports/hong-kong-green-and-sustainable-debt-market-briefing-2021.

Ministry of Economy. 2019. The Fiji Sovereign Green Bond 2019 Update. https://www.rbf.gov.fj/wp-content/uploads/2020/03/Fiji-Sovereign-Green-Bond-Impact-Report-2019.pdf.

Ministry of Economy and Finance (Italy). 2021. The MEF Publishes the Framework for the Issuance of Sovereign Green Bonds. https://www.mef.gov.it/en/ufficio-stampa/comunicati/2021/The-MEF-publishes-the-Framework-for-the-issuance-of-Sovereign-Green-Bonds-BTP-Green.-Monday-March-1st-at-3.30-p.m-00001.-CET-the-Global-Investor-Call-for-the-Framework-presentation/.

Monetary Authority of Singapore. 2023. MAS to Set Expectations on Credible Transition Planning by Financial Institutions. News release. 8 June. https://www.mas.gov.sg/news/media-releases/2023/mas-to-set-expectations-on-credible-transition-planning-by-financial-institutions.

Philippe H. Le Houérou. 2018. A Catalyst for Green Financing in Indonesia. *World Bank Blogs.* 2 August. https://blogs.worldbank.org/eastasiapacific/catalyst-green-financing-indonesia.

Prasad, A. E. Loukoianova, A. Xiaochen Feng, W. Oman. 2022. *Mobilizing Private Climate Financing in Emerging Market and Developing Economies*. IMF Staff Climate Notes. Washington, DC. https://www.imf.org/en/Publications/staff-climate-notes/Issues/2022/07/26/Mobilizing-Private-Climate-Financing-in-Emerging-Market-and-Developing-Economies-520585.

Rakhmadi, R., M. Sudirman. 2019. Developing a Guarantee Instrument to Catalyze Renewable Energy Investments in Indonesia. Climate Policy Initiative. https://climatepolicyinitiative.org/wp-content/uploads/2019/05/Developing-a-Guarantee-Instrument-to-Catalyze-Renewable-Energy-Investments-in-Indonesia.pdf.

R. Way, M. C. Ives, P. Mealy, and J. Doyne Farmer. 2022. Empirically Grounded Technology Forecasts and the Energy Transition. *Joule.* 6 (9). pp. 2057–2082. https://doi.org/10.1016/j.joule.2022.08.009.

Securities Commission Malaysia. 2022. Expansion of SRI Sukuk and Bond Grant Scheme to Facilitate Sustainable Finance. https://www.sc.com.my/resources/media/media-release/expansion-of-sri-sukuk-and-bond-grant-scheme-to-facilitate-sustainable-finance.

Securities Commission Malaysia. 2022. Principles-based Sustainable and Responsible Investment Taxonomy for the Malaysian Capital Market. Kuala Lumpur.

Securities Commission Malaysia. 2022. SC Unveils Principles-Based Sustainable and Responsible Investment Taxonomy for the Malaysian Capital Market. Kuala Lumpur. https://www.sc.com.my/resources/media/media-release/sc-unveils-principles-based-sustainable-and-responsible-investment-taxonomy-for-the-malaysian-capital-market.

S. Kidney, P. Oliver, and B. Sonerud. 2014. Greening China's Bond Market. Chapter 10 in *Greening China's Financial System*. Winnipeg: International Institute for Sustainable Development. https://www.iisd.org/system/files/publications/greening-chinas-financial-system-chapter-10.pdf.

Sustainability Insights. 2023. Asia-Pacific Sustainable Bond Issuance To Increase In 2023. 14 February. https://www.spglobal.com/_assets/documents/ratings/research/101572592.pdf.

UK Transition Plan Taskforce. 2023. *Disclosure Framework*. https://transitiontaskforce.net/disclosure-framework/.

United States 117th Congress (2021–2022), 2022. *Inflation Reduction Act of 2022*, H.R.5376, https://www.congress.gov/bill/117th-congress/house-bill/5376.

Willis Towers Watson. 2021. Asian Asset Owners: Raising Their ESG Game. ESG Beliefs and Practices Survey 2021: Asia. https://www.wtwco.com/en-hk/insights/2021/10/asian-asset-owners-raising-their-esg-game.

World Bank. 2023. *Indonesia Country Climate and Development Report*. Washington, DC: World Bank. https://www.worldbank.org/en/country/indonesia/publication/indonesia-country-climate-and-development-repo.

World Bank. 2022. *Unleashing Sustainable Finance in Southeast Asia*. Washington, DC: World Bank. https://openknowledge.worldbank.org/server/api/core/bitstreams/7ff934ad-de0a-5fd0-bed1-42e1de4f5717/content.

X. Chen, and D.L. Mauzerall. 2021. The Expanding Coal Power Fleet in Southeast Asia: Implications for Future CO2 Emissions and Electricity Generation. *Earth's Future*. 9 (12). https://doi.org/10.1029/2021EF002257.

www.ingramcontent.com/pod-product-compliance
Lightning Source LLC
Chambersburg PA
CBHW050057220326
41599CB00045B/7440